CULTURES OF THE WORLD®
MACEDONIA

Mary Lee Knowlton

BENCHMARK BOOKS

MARSHALL CAVENDISH
NEW YORK

PICTURE CREDITS
Cover: © George Spenceley/Art Directors
AFP: 5, 19, 34, 37, 39, 42, 47, 50, 51, 58, 65, 67, 91, 107, 108, 116, 118, 119, 120, 124, 128 • Alamy Images: 55, 56, 73, 96, 105, 126 • alt.TYPE/REUTERS: 63, 68, 121 • Robert Atanasovski/REUTERS: 113 • Bes Stock: 53 • Camera Press: 76, 106 • Corbis Inc.: 12, 21, 23, 48, 54, 59, 71, 97, 100, 102 • Melanie Friend/Hutchison Library: 6, 7, 11, 14, 79, 81, 99 • Getty Images: 38, 40, 41, 45, 46, 49, 62, 70, 90, 92, 94 • HBL Network Photo Agency: 13, 30, 32, 33, 35, 52, 77, 89 • Jeremy Horner/Hutchison Library: 86 • Lonely Planet Images: 3, 9, 10, 15, 16, 17, 25, 80, 88, 98, 103, 127 • MC Picture Library: 131 • Sophie Molins/Hutchison Library: 1, 60, 69, 75 • Peter Moszynski/Hutchison Library: 8, 20, 84 • National Geographic/Getty Images: 83 • North Wind Picture Archives: 22, 27 • Panos: 57, 110, 111, 115, 122 • Radu Sigheti/REUTERS: 87 • Still Pictures: 4, 18, 26, 36, 74 • STOCKFOOD/STUDIO BONISOLLI: 130 • STOCKFOOD/DAVID LOFTUS: 129 • Ognen Teofilovski/REUTERS: 43, 44, 61, 64, 66, 82, 101, 112, 114, 125 • Time Life Pictures/Getty Images: 24 • Goran Tomasevic/REUTERS: 85 • Topfoto: 28, 29, 72, 78

ACKNOWLEDGMENTS
Thanks to Gordon N. Bardos, Assistant Director, Harriman Institute, Columbia University, for his expert reading of this manuscript.

PRECEDING PAGE
Villagers dressed in traditional costumes in the Macedonian town of Stavitza.

Marshall Cavendish Benchmark
99 White Plains Road
Tarrytown, NY 10591
Website: www.marshallcavendish.us

© Marshall Cavendish International (Asia) Private Limited 2005
® "Cultures of the World" is a registered trademark of Marshall Cavendish Corporation.

Series concept and design by Times Editions
An imprint of Marshall Cavendish International (Asia) Private Limited,
A member of Times Publishing Limited

Library of Congress Cataloging-in-Publication Data
Knowlton, MaryLee, 1946-
    Macedonia / by MaryLee Knowlton.
      p. cm. — (Cultures of the world)
    Includes bibliographical references and index.
    ISBN 0-7614-1854-7
    1. Macedonia (Republic)—Juvenile literature. I. Title. II. Series.
    DR2160.K6 2005
    949.76—dc22   2004022735

Printed in China

7 6 5 4 3 2 1

CONTENTS

A church in Ohrid, Macedonia's historic city.

Macedonians in Skopje.

INTRODUCTION

MACEDONIA IS ONE of the newest nations in the world, admitted to the United Nations in 1993, and yet its name is the oldest surviving name of a country in Europe. The ancient Macedonians had their own language, culture, and ethnic makeup.

Today's Macedonia has a constitution that carefully proclaims the equal rights of people of all ethnic backgrounds and cultures. These contrasts between ancient history and contemporary reality make Macedonia a challenging place to live in, and endow its people with verve and grit and a very wide frame of reference.

This volume of *Cultures of the World* presents the people and the culture of Macedonia in all their complexity and richness.

GEOGRAPHY

IN HISTORICAL TERMS, today's Macedonia occupies the territory of the western half of the ancient kingdom of Macedonia, north of Helles, west of Thrace, and east of Illyria. In contemporary geographical terms, it shares the Balkan Peninsula with Albania, Greece, and its compatriots in the former Yugoslavia. Both the historical and the contemporary geographical definitions of the country have shaped Macedonia's political reality.

Macedonia is a tiny country, smaller than the state of Vermont, with an area of 9,928 square miles (25,713 square km). It is landlocked in the middle of the Balkan Peninsula with Albania to its west and Greece to the south. The Sar Planina Mountains in the northwest form the border with Albania, Kosovo, and Serbia. To the northeast of Macedonia lies Bulgaria.

MOUNTAINS

Macedonia is a country of high points with 34 mountains that are higher than 6,562 feet (2,000 m). The tallest is Mount Golem Korab at 9,032 feet (2,753 m) above sea level. In the Sar Planina mountain range, Titov Vrv is 9,016 feet (2,748 m) high and Turchin reaches 8,865 feet (2,702 m).

Titov Vrv means "Tito's Mountain," and was named after (and by) the former leader of Yugoslavia. Though it is the second highest mountain in Macedonia, it is the highest mountain lying completely within the country and within Yugoslavia, which is why it was picked to honor Tito.

Above: **Mountain scenery near Tetovo.**

Opposite: **A section of the homes near the waterfront in Ohrid.**

7

Lake Ohrid, the Balkan Peninsula's deepest lake.

WATERWAYS

The Vardar, 187 miles (301 km) long, is Macedonia's most significant river in both size and history, cutting across the middle of the country from the northwest to the southeast where it flows into Greece and empties into the Aegean Sea. The Treska and the Crun rivers branch off the Vardar on its way south through the country, the Treska at Skopje and the Crun farther south.

The Republic of Macedonia has 53 natural or artificial lakes. Lake Ohrid in the southwest, with a depth of 938 feet (286 m), is the deepest lake on the Balkan Peninsula and is part of both Macedonia and Albania. Of its area of 130 square miles (340 sq km), about a third belongs to Albania. Over three million years old, Lake Ohrid is often called a living museum of living fossils. Lake Ohrid is largely a spring-fed lake, drawing its waters from deep underground, rather than from contributory rivers. Its waters are fully replaced only every 60 years, which makes it particularly vulnerable to damage by pollution.

The lake is home to the endangered Ohrid trout, a fish from the Tertiary period of geological history. It is also the only sanctuary for other endangered fish that exist only in fossil form in other parts of the world where they became extinct during the Ice Age. Overfishing and pollution have increased the peril for these rare creatures.

Lake Prespa, a little farther south, is part of both Albania and Macedonia and also part of Greece. Lake Dojran, in the southeast, is on the Greek border. Fishermen pull about 1,650 tons of fish each year from Macedonian lakes and rivers.

Lake Prespa, the second largest lake in Macedonia.

CLIMATE

Macedonia is a country of hot, dry summers and falls. Its winters, though snowy between November and February, are warmer than its neighbors' to the north, thanks to the moderating Aegean winds that blow from the south through the Vardar River valley. Still, in the mountainous areas, farmers can see snow on the mountain peaks when they plant their seeds in the warmer valleys in the spring.

NATIONAL PARKS AND WORLD HERITAGE SITES

Macedonia has three national parks, all in the western part of the country. Galicica comprises the land area between Lakes Ohrid and Prespa. To the east of Lake Prespa is Pelister Park. North of the city of Debar on the Albanian border is Mavrovo. Lake Ohrid has World Heritage status, but

Lake Ohrid, home to more than 140 endemic species, is a UNESCO World Heritage Site.

UNESCO, the United Nations organization that designates locations as worthy of the status, has expressed disapproval of the way the lake is being managed and is reevaluating the designation.

The best known summer resorts are in Ohrid, Prespa, and Dojran. In winter the mountain resorts of Popova Shapka, Mavrovo, Pelister, Krushevo, and Ponikva draw skiers from all over Europe. Among the better known spas are those of Bansko (Strumica), Debar, Negorci (Gevgelija), and Kechovica (Shtip).

LAND USE

Nearly 35 percent of the land of Macedonia is forested, 27 percent is arable agricultural land, and another 27 percent is pastureland. Over 70 percent of the arable land is privately owned, mostly in small parcels.

The Sar Mountains, located above the city of Tetovo.

Macedonia is a country of hunters, over 30,000 of them. Animals for sport hunting include deer, bears, hares, boars, partridges, and pheasants. Hunting grounds and reserves are set aside for hunters.

FLORA AND FAUNA

Macedonia is a land of forests. In the mountain regions, beech and chestnut trees grow in the lower elevations. Above 3,937 feet (1,200 m), conifers prevail, mostly fir and pine. Around Lakes Ohrid and Prespa, cypress, walnut, and fig trees grow.

The forests are home to deer, martens, and wild boars. In the mountains, there are bears, ibexes, lynx, and chamois. The western lake district has a wide variety of fish and water fowl, including cormorants, the Ohrid trout, and pelicans.

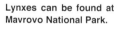

Lynxes can be found at Mavrovo National Park.

CITIES

SKOPJE Macedonia's capital city is located in the north of the country in a valley on the Vardar River. Skopje has been a city since 500 B.C. and served several civilizations as the intersection of two trading routes.

The Vardar divides the city into ethnic communities, the Muslim section on the north bank and the Orthodox Christian on the south. The Muslim section of town, the old city, has a traditional Turkish bazaar every day, where people can buy fresh foods in season and Macedonian crafts. The southern part of the city contains the buildings of the government as well as shopping malls, modern hotels, and Internet cafés.

Skopje, Macedonia's capital city, is also its largest.

The architecture of Skopje reflects its numerous rulers, who embarked on building projects each time the city changed hands. Beautiful old mosques, a stone bridge known as Kameni Most, and medieval Turkish baths have survived floods and earthquakes. An earthquake in 1963, which left more than 1,000 people dead and 100,000 homeless, destroyed most of the city's 18th- and 19th-century buildings in the southern part of the city, while sparing the Turkish buildings in the north.

The church and monastery of Sveti Spas, which means "holy salvation," has survived both earthquakes and communism as the only remaining monastery in Skopje. Parts of the church date to the 14th century, and additions and repairs extended into the 19th. During the 400 years of

The Mustafa Pasha mosque in Skopje was built in the 15th century.

Ottoman rule, a church could not be built taller than a mosque, so the additions to Sveti Spas were built underground.

OHRID The city of Ohrid is a treasure not only to Macedonia but to the rest of the world as well. Cultural and environmental importance has earned both the city and the lake on which it is sited UNESCO protection. As one of the world's oldest lakes, Lake Ohrid rates protection because of its supply of ancient and rare animal life. The city itself has an ancient history as well, stretching back to prehistoric times, around 6000 B.C. Once known as Lihnidos, which means city of light, Ohrid has been home to most of the important peoples of the area, including Illyrians, Greeks, and Romans as well as Macedonians.

At the end of the ninth century, it was renamed Ohrid, meaning city of a hill, by the Slavs who had taken control. Since then Ohrid has been the heart of Macedonia, originating its written language, its first university, its church, and many of its rebellions against invaders and occupiers. In

Ohrid is one of Europe's oldest human settlements and was made a World Heritage Site in 1979.

Windows of the Church of Saint Sophia.

1466 the citizens of Ohrid sided with the Albanians and their leader, George Skenderbeg, in their revolt against the Ottoman Empire. Though the revolt was ultimately put down, the effort was a noble one, and Macedonians of Albanian descent in Ohrid still cherish Skenderbeg's memory.

Throughout the city of Ohrid, its history as a trading crossroad and a center of many civilizations is evident in the architecture that remains, sometimes in ruin, but treasured nevertheless. The Church of Saint Sophia illustrates a history typical of Macedonia. In the early 11th century it was built as a cathedral for the archbishop on the remains of a former basilica. Under the Ottomans it was transformed into a mosque, and later, though still during the Ottoman Empire, it became a warehouse. In 1912 it became, once again, a church. In its incarnation as a cathedral, the church was lavishly decorated with frescoes on its walls and ceiling. As Islam forbids human representation, the frescoes were painted over during the building's mosque incarnation, and so they remained until the 20th century, when they were restored to their original beauty.

Ohrid is very much a lake community, and people get around by boat taxi as well as car and bus. In summer it is host to the Ohrid International Swimming Marathon, a 19-mile (30-km) race from Saint Naum on the Albanian border to the city of Ohrid.

BITOLA Bitola is Macedonia's second largest city, with a population of 80,000 people. It is in the southeastern corner of the country and was a stop on the Via Egnatia, the Roman road that connected Constantinople (now Istanbul) with Rome. It was founded by the father of Alexander the Great, and at one time every European country of importance had a consulate there. It has since lost much of its international glory, but retains

Cruise ships at the Ohrid harbor.

its cultural significance, which is evident in the buildings that are well preserved throughout the city. Bitola was central to the Ilinden uprising in 1903 as the training center for guerillas. During the brutal reprisals that the Turks visited upon the Macedonians after the uprising was subdued, the Manaki brothers, Janaki and Milton, established a photography studio in Bitola and recorded for all the world to see the violence of those years and of the Balkan Wars that followed in 1912–13.

TETOVO Tetovo is in the northwestern part of Macedonia, not far from Kosovo and Albania at the foot of the towering Mount Titov Vrv. It is the most important Albanian city in Macedonia, and it is the headquarters for

Bitola, Macedonia's second largest city.

the Albanian political parties. The language of the streets and shops is Albanian, and though Macedonian is spoken, it is not favored.

With its Albanian majority, the city of Tetovo challenges the Macedonian government to live up to its claims to multiethnic tolerance and participation. In the late 1990s and at the start of the 21st century, Tetovo's citizens struggled for the right to provide education in the Albanian language, especially at the university level. Only with international help were they successful in establishing the South East European University (SEEU). Of 3,800 students who studied in the university in 2003, nearly 3,000 spoke Albanian as their first language. Today a second Albanian-language university, Tetovo University, offers courses and has been granted recognition and accreditation from the Macedonian government.

Friday prayers at a mosque in Tetovo.

HISTORY

THE STATE OF MACEDONIA that was created in 1991 was carved out of lands that had for centuries been home to peoples of varying ethnicities, creeds, and traditions. Within the new state, people trace their identity through differing histories formed by when they came and where they came from.

MACEDONIA'S MYTHIC ORIGINS

Early Greek writers describe a mythical country called Paeonia that stretched the length of the Vardar River, from its origins in the mountains of the north through today's Greece to the Aegean Sea.

According to Homer, the Paeons were descended from Axios, the Greek river god and were participants in the Trojan War. The Paeons and neighboring tribes, who were the ancestors of Greeks, Albanians, Bulgarians, and Serbs, fought alongside and against each other in the Balkans for centuries. The remains of their walled cities remain throughout Macedonia. Their civilization, the first in the area, flourished between 7000 and 3500 B.C.

ANCIENT MACEDONIA

To the land of Paeonia, legend continues, came Macedon, a son (and grandson) of Zeus, child of his first daughter. The Macedonians were mountain people, fierce hunters and fighters, and boisterous drinkers and dancers. The first known king of Macedonia was Caranus (also called Charon) who ruled from 808 to 778 B.C. and established a kingdom that

Above: **The mosaic floor of the House of Psalms in the ancient town of Stobi, which dates to the sixth century** B.C.

Opposite: **The medieval Church of Sveti Stefan.**

A painting of the king of India surrendering to Alexander the Great.

lasted for 400 years. The Macedonian kingdom expanded during the 700 years that followed, from the reign of Caranus through 21 more kings, reaching its peak during the reign of Alexander the Great. Under Alexander, Macedonia covered the lands of today's Macedonia, Egypt and other parts of the Middle East, the Aegean Islands, and parts of Iran and India.

Alexander's early and sudden death in 323 B.C. left the Macedonian Empire without a strong leader, and it fell into political and military disarray as rival leaders competed for power. Over the next 150 years the Roman Empire waged war three times against the Macedonians, who were being fragmented and weakened. In 168 B.C. the Romans decisively defeated the last Macedonian king, Perseus, and took dominion over Macedonia.

Rome was determined that the Macedonian Empire would not rise again and to that end divided it into four autonomous regions. Each region was free to determine its own course, electing a magistrate and passing laws. Significantly, though, the regions could not trade or enter into alliances with each other, thus assuring Rome that they would neither cooperate in any uprisings or unite into one nation.

Throughout the 800 years that followed, Rome expanded its empire throughout Europe and Asia. As a crossroad of trading routes, Macedonia was crucial to the empire and towns, roads, economies, and Christianity stabilized the region.

For nearly 100 years beginning in the mid-fifth century, Huns, Goths, and Avars laid waste to the Roman cities of Macedonia. What they did not ruin, an earthquake in A.D. 518 destroyed. The people of Macedonia downsized once more, forming small mountain communities centered on their churches. Their former international trading economy was reduced to subsistence farming.

The ruins of a synagogue in Stobi are evidence of Jewish presence in the country in the third century.

The core of the infantry during Philip II's reign was the Macedonian phalanx.

Roving Slavic tribes moved into the vacuum created by the defeat of the Romans and the loose authority of the Bulgarians who had nominal rule. Taking advantage of the disunity in the region, they settled in the northern reaches of Macedonia. Over the next 300 years, they took Macedonia as their homeland, intermarrying and converting to Christianity, but preserving their own language. In 976 they proclaimed one of their own king of Bulgaria. King Samuel ruled until 1015, during which time the new kingdom developed its own church and a written language in which to conduct services.

The reign of King Samuel was not peaceful. The Bulgarians gave only half-hearted effort to retaining their rule, besieged in their own land by the ascending forces of the Byzantine Empire, to which they finally fell. The conquering Byzantines were more engaged, however, and warred ceaselessly against the Bulgarian kingdom Samuel had based in what is today Macedonia. When they finally defeated King Samuel's troops in 1014, they took the added precaution of blinding his surviving 15,000 soldiers, leaving only one eye for 100 men so they could find their way home. The march home took over two months. When King Samuel caught sight of his blinded and battered army staggering towards him, he suffered a heart attack and died days later.

The Byzantines ruled Macedonia till the beginning of the 14th century when the Ottoman Empire defeated them throughout their lands. During this time Macedonia played reluctant host to Norman raiders and Christian Crusaders as well as paying taxes and serving in the armies of the Byzantine conquerors.

The interior of a Byzantine church in Ohrid.

The stone bridge over the Vardar river, known as the Kameni Most. It was rebuilt by the Turks in the 15th century.

By 1394 Ottoman control of Macedonia was complete and would remain absolute for the next 500 years. In Macedonia, as elsewhere in the Balkan lands, uprisings occurred, but they were never longlasting or successful, and were savagely put down. The Turks reestablished towns and trade, introduced Islam and its legal system, and Turkish architecture and art. Through Turkish forbearance and Macedonian persistence, however, Macedonian culture maintained its hold on its people through the unifying influences of Christianity and language.

The 19th century was a time of great ethnic and nationalistic fervor in Macedonia. Macedonia's neighbors Greece, Bulgaria, and Serbia, newly liberated from the Turks, turned their attentions and aspirations toward Macedonia. They opened schools, promoted their languages and religions, and influenced the Turks in developing roads and railway routes to their countries. The Greeks and Bulgarians also sent roving bands of guerillas to use force and fear to convince the Macedonians to reconsider their national loyalty and ethnic identity.

ALEXANDER AND THE GORDION KNOT

The oracle had foretold that the future king of Phrygia would appear to his people riding in a wagon. So when Gordius, a simple peasant, arrived in the village square in an oxcart, they proclaimed him their king. Gordius dedicated his oxcart to Zeus as tribute, and tied it up with an elaborate knot, tucking the ends inside. The oracle spoke again, saying that whoever untied the knot would rule all of Asia. For over 100 years people tried to untie the knot with no success. When Alexander arrived in Phrygia, which had been renamed Gordion, he was just 23 and had yet to earn the respect of his troops. Solving the puzzle posed by the Gordian knot was a challenge he could not resist.

With his troops looking on, Alexander struggled to loosen the knot with his hands, but could not decipher its twists. In frustration, he drew his sword, saying, "What difference does it make how I loosen it?" and with one blow he cut the rope.

That night the Gods signaled their approval with a great display of lightning and thunder, and Alexander went on to rule all of Asia.

People have long debated whether Alexander cheated or at least violated the spirit of the contest, or whether it is in fact possible to tie a knot that cannot be untied. Mathematicians have since then tried to devise such a knot. Many theories abound. Here is one: Fold a circular length of rope and tie two multiple overhand knots in it. Then pass the end loops over the entangled central part. Then shrink the rope until it is tight. Now the end parts of the rope are too short to pass over the inner part. If the only way to tie a knot that cannot be untied is to shrink the rope after tying it, Alexander did not cheat. But maybe there is another way. The debate will continue as long as the search for the knot goes on.

ALEXANDER AND HIS HORSE

Legend says that Alexander's beloved horse, Bucephalus, was a gift to his father, Philip II. When no one could tame the horse, 12-year-old Alexander took up the challenge. His father was angry at this display of pride and considered it an insult to the warriors who had already tried and failed to ride the horse. He told his son that if he failed he would have to pay the price of the horse, a large amount of money that Alexander would have had difficulty raising. But Alexander had noticed that when others tried to ride Bucephalus, the horse seemed to be afraid of his shadow. So he took the horse out into sunlight with his shadow behind him, whispered soothingly in his ear, and peaceably mounted him. When he rode him past his father and dismounted, his father wept tears of joy and said, according to Plutarch, "O my son, look thee out a kingdom equal to and worthy of thyself, for Macedonia is too little for thee."

Bucephalus and Alexander rode in hundreds of battles and thousands of miles, partners in every battle Alexander fought in Greece and Asia. When the horse died of wounds received during a battle in India in 326 B.C., Alexander held a grand funeral and named a city in his honor.

INDEPENDENCE

With the Turks still in control of their country and their neighbors beating on the doors, Macedonians in the second half of the 19th century began to organize.

The first stage of organization was a development of national consciousness. To that end education and literature flourished, and the people became literate and aware of their own identity. Soon revolutionary leaders emerged, and uprisings against the Turks in 1876 and 1878, though unsuccessful in their aim, raised the desire for national independence and solidified the movement. In 1893 the Internal Macedonian Revolutionary

"Those who believe that the answer of our national liberation lies in Bulgaria, Serbia or Greece might consider themselves a good Bulgarian, good Serb or a good Greek, but not a good Macedonian."

—*Grotse Delchev*

Revolutionaries getting a briefing from their leader in 1903.

The Vardar region in Macedonia has been batted about among several countries.

Organization (IMRO) emerged with Grotse Delchev as its leader and "Macedonia for the Macedonians" as its slogan. In 1903 the IMRO declared Macedonian independence on August 2. The Turks reacted immediately and brutally, suppressing the revolt. But the Macedonians had grabbed international attention. Though the revolt was unsuccessful, Macedonians look to the date of the proclamation, August 2, 1903, as the symbolic beginning of their nation.

International intervention resulted in the division of Macedonia. The Turks were out, but the neighbors were in. The largest part, the Aegean region, went to Greece, which called it "Northern Greece." The Pirin region in the east went to Bulgaria, which abolished the Macedonian name. The Vardar region to the north went to Serbia, and it was renamed Southern Serbia. The leaders of Greece and Serbia agreed on a border: Only Serbs lived to the north of the border, only Greeks to the south, and

Macedonians theoretically no longer existed. All three former neighbors imposed their identity on the Macedonians, either denying their ethnicity entirely or treating them as inferior in an attempt to encourage their assimilation. Greece was particularly intent on obliterating all signs of Macedonian history by changing names of villages, rivers, mountains, and other geographical locations. Macedonians were forced to renounce their names and take Greek-sounding names and were forbidden to speak their own language.

The Macedonian parcels of land continued to be batted about throughout the first half of the 20th century. During World War I, Bulgaria occupied the Vardar region that had been Serbia's. But when the war ended with Bulgaria on the losing side, Serbia got it back. The powers that carved Europe into new nations at the Paris Peace Conference in 1918 ignored Macedonian pleas for a united and independent nation. Instead they made Vardar Macedonia a part of the newly-proclaimed kingdom of the Serbs, Croats, and Slovenes, which later became Yugoslavia.

Between the two world wars, Macedonians in all three countries worked to unite their nation once again, but to no avail. The governments

When Delchev was beheaded in 1903, his head was mounted on a post on Kameni Most and later lost. The body was buried in and, to the Macedonian way of thinking, rested uneasily until 1964, when it was exhumed and reinterred in Skopje in the Church of Sveti Spas.

BALKANIZE — THE EVOLUTION OF A WORD

When Yugoslavia was created after World War I from the territories inhabited by various Balkan peoples, a new verb was created as well: *balkanize*. More than half a century later the meaning of *balkanize* as the creation of small, mutually hostile states or territories is the same in languages throughout the world. Macedonia is one of the Balkan states gathered into Yugoslavia, and then separated in 1991 when it proclaimed its independence. When people use the word *balkanize*, whether to refer to factions within a country, a government, or even a family, one thing is clear: those within the *balkanized* entity are not going to be getting along well at all.

of Greece, Serbia, and Bulgaria were very strong and oppressive, and Macedonian nationalism came at a high price to its participants. But literary activity flourished and, in Vienna, expatriates began to organize for the day when they could go home to a free and united Macedonia.

When World War II broke out, Bulgaria once again took over all of the former Macedonia, including the Vardar and Aegean regions. Allied with the Nazis, they collaborated in sending the Jews of Salonica to their deaths. But by 1943 the Macedonian communists were gaining strength and sympathy for their desire to throw the Bulgarians out. They formed the Communist Party of Macedonia, established an army, and set up local and national liberation councils. When, as in World War I, it developed that

The town of Kumanovo in northern Macedonia in the 1930s.

Bulgaria had chosen the losing side, they were driven out of the lands they occupied. In April, 1945 the Macedonian resistance founded the first Macedonian government, a free state within the Yugoslav Federation. Macedonians from all three parts of the divided country celebrated, although only the Vardar lands were affected. The free state was called the People's Republic of Macedonia.

In 1991 the Federation of Yugoslavia began to dissolve during the general collapse of communism in Europe. Slovenia, Croatia, and Bosnia declared their independence. On September 8, Macedonians voted to declare their independence as well and proclaimed themselves the Independent Republic of Macedonia. Kiro Gligorov was elected the first president. In 1993 Macedonia was admitted to the United Nations.

The years since independence have been challenging. Initially Greece's hostility toward the new country was very damaging as it imposed a trade embargo and pressured other European countries not to do business with Macedonia. Furthermore, despite the constitution's declaration of ethnic equality, some of Macedonia's ethnic minorities, in particular the Albanians, felt that they were being unfairly represented. These problems combined with general unrest in the area to create an unstable and unsafe environment for many of Macedonia's people.

Intervention and aid from international organizations and foreign countries has done much to stabilize Macedonia. Greece has lifted its embargo, and the two countries are embarking tentatively on projects and trade of mutual benefit.

The first president of independent Macedonia, Kiro Gligorov.

MACEDONIANS IN GREECE

The lot of Macedonians in Greece has been especially difficult. When World War II ended, Aegean Macedonia reverted to Greece. Once again the Macedonian language was forbidden. Macedonians were imprisoned, murdered, and tortured by the thousands. Their villages were pillaged and abandoned. During the civil war in Greece that was fought between the army and the communists from 1946 to 1949, Macedonians fought the military dictatorship on the side of the communists, who promised them their rights. For two years they comprised half of the communist forces, and were rewarded with schools, newspapers, and activities in their own language and according to their customs. But the United States and Britain gave support to the army dictatorship to prevent another communist government in Europe, and the communists were defeated. The retaliation against the Macedonians by the victorious army was catastrophic. Thousands of families were torn apart as people sent their children abroad to safety, and villages were once more burned to the ground.

Greece even resisted the attempts of Vardar Macedonia to reconstitute itself as Macedonia, claiming that Greece had the sole right to the name of Macedonia. When in 1993 Macedonia was recognized by the United Nations as an independent nation, Greek pressure resulted in an official name for the country of Former Yugoslav Republic of Macedonia (FYROM).

MACEDONIANS IN BULGARIA

Beginning with Pirin Macedonia's first assignment to Bulgaria, national identity was a point of contention. Initially Bulgaria simply refused to acknowledge that there were Macedonians within its borders, maintaining that everyone was a Bulgarian. Expressions of Macedonian heritage were rigorously opposed. Throughout the fluctuations of the first half of the 20th century, opposition and denial remained standard Bulgarian practice. With the communist accession in 1946, however, the Macedonians were recognized as a separate nationality. For the next 10 years, the majority of people in Pirin Macedonia identified themselves as Macedonian. Schools operated in the Macedonian language and taught Macedonian history. Newpapers, theaters, and bookstores thrived. Artists' collectives spread the Macedonian culture and literary language.

Then in 1956, the Bulgarian government changed its approach to the Macedonian question once again and forbade any expression of Macedonian culture. By 1965 only 1 percent of the population of Pirin Macedonia identified itself as Macedonian. No one doubts that the population of Pirin Macedonia is still largely Macedonian, but the official census says otherwise. In recent years, with the loosening of totalitarian rule in Bulgaria, Macedonians have once again been asserting their identity.

GOVERNMENT

AS FEDERAL YUGOSLAVIA was disintegrating at the beginning of the 1990s, 95 percent of voting Macedonians approved the independence and sovereignty of the Republic of Macedonia on September 8, 1991. The new constitution declared the Republic of Macedonia a sovereign, independent, civil, and democratic state, and it recognized the complete equality of the Macedonians and all ethnic minorities.

It read ". . . Macedonia is constituted as a national country of the Macedonian people which guarantees complete civil equality and permanent mutual living of the Macedonian people with the Albanians, Turks, Vlachs, Roma, and the other nationalities living in the Republic of Macedonia."

On April 8, 1993, the Republic of Macedonia was unanimously and with acclamation admitted to the United Nations as its 181st member.

THE CONSTITUTION

On November 17, 1991, Macedonia adopted the new Constitution of the Republic of Macedonia. The constitution guarantees the rule of law, a democratic political system, and individual rights.

The values the government and the people of Macedonia aspire to are encoded in the constitution. Among these values are: the right to vote for all citizens over 18, the protection of property from unlawful seizure, the right to artistic and political expression, freedom to conduct and own

Above: **Swearing-in ceremony in June 2004 to usher in Hari Kostov as Macedonia's Prime Minister.**

Opposite: **Parliament in session in Skopje.**

37

business, political pluralism, free expression of national identity, and respect for international law.

THE PRESIDENT The president is elected directly by a majority vote of the people to a term of five years and may serve two terms. Working within the limits of the constitution, the president has the following powers and responsibilities: negotiating international agreements; appointing ambassadors and envoys to foreign countries; receiving foreign diplomatic representatives; appointing three members to the Security Council; appointing members to the Council of Inter-Ethnic Relations, two judges of the Constitutional Court, and two members of the Republican Judicial Council; as well as other duties defined by the Constitution. The person holding the office of president is also head of the armed forces, representative of the country at home and abroad, and the head of the Macedonian Security Council. The office confers immunity from prosecution and requires the president to report to the parliament once a year on the state of the country.

THE PARLIAMENT The legislative branch of the government is called the Assembly, which is

composed of 120 directly elected representatives of the people who serve four-year terms. Critical to the election of the Assembly is the constitutionally guaranteed right of people to form political parties. In the first election held in 1990, for example, 17 parties were represented by 1,157 candidates for the 120 offices. Under the old Yugoslav system, though people voted for their representatives, they were restricted in their choices to candidates who supported the communist regime. The present system allows small constituencies to form alliances with larger parties and thereby exercise some power. In the 2002 elections, 22 of the 120 seats in the parliament were filled by women, one of them an Albanian woman.

The duties of the Assembly include adopting and interpreting laws, adopting a budget and spending the money collected, ratifying international agreements, declaring war and peace, electing and dismissing judges and

Above: **A minute's silence is observed at the memorial service of late Macedonian president Boris Trajkovski, who died in a plane crash in February 2004.**

Opposite: **The president of Macedonia, Branko Crvenkovski.**

A woman casts her vote during Macedonia's parliamentary elections in September 2002.

holders of other offices, and electing the government of the Republic of Macedonia. Any member of the Assembly can propose a law. In addition, a law can be introduced by a petition signed by 10,000 voters. Laws are passed by a majority of 50 percent of the representatives. The president of the republic can veto the law, which can be returned for another vote. If the law then passes by a margin of two-thirds, the president is required to sign it into law.

The parliament is headed by a president elected by 61 or more of the assembly members for a term of four years. The parliamentary president's duties are to run the governmental sessions and see that the rules of parliamentary procedure are followed. If the president of the republic is unable to govern, the president of the parliament takes over that office.

THE JUDICIARY Judges are elected to unrestricted terms of office by the parliament. Macedonia has 31 courts: 27 courts of the first instance, 3 courts of appeal, and a supreme court. Additionally, there is the Constitutional

Court, which is charged with ensuring that there is no conflict of interest or abuse of power among the three branches of the government. The constitution of Macedonia specifically prohibits the creation of any emergency or other special court. This prohibition reflects on Macedonia's history as part of Yugoslavia, when secret, military, or special government courts operated as part of a system of government oppression.

LOCAL GOVERNMENT

Local governments are elected by citizens of municipalities. These governments can collect taxes to finance the municipality, though the republic also provides funds. Citizens participate in their local governments

Supporters of a Macedonian opposition party celebrate victory after election results are announced.

Officers from a multi-ethnic police force greet ethnic Albanian children in Matejca.

both directly and through their elected representatives. The level of participation often depends on the size of the municipality, with people in villages and smaller towns being more directly involved. Governmental issues such as urban planning, communal activities, sports, childcare, preschool education, primary education, and basic healthcare are usually decided at the local level.

AN ETHNIC DILEMMA

Ethnic Macedonians and ethnic Albanians in the Republic of Macedonia have distinctly different but equally ethnocentric views of the causes and course of armed conflict that raged between them in 2001. These attitudes have impeded efforts to diminish animosities and have the potential for fueling further violence.

The fighting between armed Albanians and Macedonian security forces in 2001 ended in August of that year when they signed the Framework Agreement at Ohrid. In September the voters passed amendments to the constitution, which gave greater recognition to the Albanian language and greater power to local Albanian minorities. Since then many of Macedonia's political leaders have vowed to develop cooperation between the two ethnic communities. A daunting challenge facing the country is to find a way to promote cooperation at the social level, as well as the political, between groups that have been separated by language, religion, and culture. Today most education is segregated, with the two groups not inclined to see any benefits to educating children together. The way the conflict of 2001 is presented to students and interpreted in the curriculum at all levels of education will significantly influence the course of ethnic relations.

Ethnic Albanians stage a protest in Struga to demand the release of fellow Albanians imprisoned during the ethnic conflict of 2001.

INTERNATIONAL AFFAIRS

Macedonia is hopeful that it will be admitted into membership in NATO, the North Atlantic Treaty Organization, in 2007. NATO membership confers both responsibility and protection on its members, and, in the cases of Macedonia and other emerging countries in Eastern Europe and the Balkans, international recognition and validation.

The government of Macedonia has given both voice and physical support to the wars in Iraq and Afghanistan, contributing its troops to both fronts and indicating that they will send more if asked. A 31-man team of professional soldiers known as Wolves was responsible for the arrest of three of the 55 most-wanted members of Saddam Hussein's inner circle. The soldiers were also awarded medals by the American government for

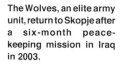

The Wolves, an elite army unit, return to Skopje after a six-month peace-keeping mission in Iraq in 2003.

saving the lives of four American troops. The Macedonian government hoped that its participation in what the Americans called "the coalition of the willing" would result in American support for Macedonia's bid for membership in NATO. By 2004 the Americans had already rewarded Macedonia's participation with $9 million to buy military supplies.

But Macedonia's participation as a coalition member in the war against Iraq had deadly consequences for several Macedonians from the city of Kumanovo. In August 2004, three Macedonians working for an American company in Iraq were abducted by Iraqis who opposed the American-led presence in their country and accused the men of being spies. In October, the kidnappers claimed to have killed the hostages and sent a videotape of the bodies to Al-Jazeera, a television station in Qatar. The opportunity to work in Iraq had been especially attractive to men, many of them construction workers, from the town of Kumanovo where unemployment had left many families mired in poverty. Even after the deaths of the hostages, recruiters for American companies found Kumanovo's workers willing to go to Iraq.

There is disagreement among parliamentarians on this issue. Some have been reluctant to increase their commitment, saying that their agreement was based on the belief that they would be contributing to a peacekeeping, postwar effort, only to find that they are engaged in active warfare. At the same time, Macedonians recognize that their participation in these wars exposes them to retaliatory terrorist attacks.

Unfortunately for the Macedonian people, terrorist activity in this arena has been committed by the government itself. In 2002 the government proclaimed that it had captured and killed six Pakistanis and one Indian intent on committing terrorist acts. In 2004, however, the

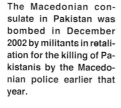

The Macedonian consulate in Pakistan was bombed in December 2002 by militants in retaliation for the killing of Pakistanis by the Macedonian police earlier that year.

Prime Minister Hari Kostov hands over his shotgun during the 45-day disarming operation in 2003.

government admitted that it had tricked the innocent men into entering their country with promises to help them pass into Western Europe where they could find work. Once the immigrants were in Macedonia, the government forces ambushed them, murdering them and planting weapons near their dead bodies. The interior minister who ordered the murders fled to Croatia.

TOWARD A MORE PEACEFUL SOCIETY

At the end of 2003, residents of Macedonia turned over nearly 8,000 illegal weapons—from rocket launchers to assault rifles—during an amnesty program that gave people 45 days to voluntarily disarm.

In all, authorities collected 55 rocket launchers, 247 land mines, 348 AK-47s, close to 800 hand grenades, 3,590 rifles, 2,794 handguns, over 1,000 detonators for explosives, and more than 100,000 rounds of ammunition. Most of the weapons were collected in areas of recent armed conflict, offering hope that people were not going to resume fighting.

ECONOMY

WHEN MACEDONIA DECLARED ITS INDEPENDENCE in 1991, it was already the poorest and least developed republic in Yugoslavia. Its economy was part of the centrally planned economy of a now collapsed union. The Yugoslav plan had assigned to Macedonia the role of building and running plants for heavy industry, which have since collapsed with the loss of their partners in the former Yugoslav republics.

The years that followed further weakened its economy. No longer did it receive aid from a central government, trade was restricted by an embargo imposed on Serbia, Greece imposed an embargo on Macedonia, Albania's even weaker economy left it unsuitable as a trading partner, and Bulgaria nursed bad feelings toward the new republic, making it disinclined to trade with Macedonia. War conditions in Kosovo through 2001 limited international investment and participation in Macedonia as well.

Despite all this, the economy in Macedonia has improved since 2001, and continued growth seems to be in its future. The rate of inflation is low, and Macedonia's currency has been stable.

As a Yugoslav republic, Macedonia had a communist economy, with state ownership of property and industry. Since 1991, however, much of the industry has been transferred to private ownership. The government has invested in roads, airports, railways, and hydroelectric plants. Trade prospects with Bulgaria, Greece, Serbia, and Albania have improved since the cessation of hostilities and lifting of embargoes.

Above: **A shoeshine worker on the streets of Skopje.**

Opposite: **A power station in central Macedonia.**

49

EMPLOYMENT

The Macedonian government counts about 450,000 employed workers, 170,000 of them women. Nearly 100,000 work in industry and mining. Agriculture employs about 35,000; building 42,000; trade 47,000; education, culture, and the media about 35,000; and the health services about 34,000.

As in any developing economy, unemployment is a grave problem, bringing with it social and political problems as well as economic. In Macedonia the unemployed comprise nearly one-third of the working population, numbering over 170,000. Of these, nearly three-fourths have never held a job. Many of the never-employed are young people and, as

Workers in a grocery store take a break. About half a million people in Macedonia are employed.

in other Balkan countries, the result of unemployment has been a wave of migration to the United States and more prosperous European countries, where employment is a more likely and lucrative prospect. A black market trade in human beings and drugs has further blighted the economy and the society.

A metal plant worker in Skopje. Macedonia's metal exports include zinc, iron, and steel.

INDUSTRY

Macedonia once supplied much of Yugoslavia with hydroelectric power, but today it barely supplies enough for its own use. Much more capacity will be required to support industry, which is also underdeveloped. The Macedonian government hopes that increased international aid to rebuild Macedonia's hydroelectric industry will also result in industrial partnerships. Today it has a small textile industry and also exports iron and zinc. It imports nearly twice as much as it exports. Because its industry is both primarily low technology and comparatively high-cost labor, it is at a disadvantage in competition with countries like China and India.

A tobacco plantation in the Vardar region.

AGRICULTURE

Macedonia's southern climate and abundant water resources make it suitable for growing a wide variety of crops. Tomatoes, peppers, corn, grapes, rice, tobacco, and wheat thrive on small family farms reclaimed from the large communist-owned collectives. Because of a lack of large-scale refrigeration and shipping systems, however, farmers are still unable to make trade a part of their industry, and the agriculture industry suffers from being able to supply only what is in season. The grape industry is beginning to overcome some of these drawbacks as wineries develop near vineyards, and wine is becoming a successful Macedonian industry and export.

In the past, tobacco was one of Macedonia's main exports, and tobacco sheds with their drying racks are scattered throughout the countryside. But it is tobacco with a heavy tar content, and the trend towards lighter tar cigarettes has reduced its appeal.

Farming in Macedonia is very labor intensive. On many farms, animals rather than machines still pull the plows and the market wagons. Farming on the terraced lands of the mountains can be a community project, as people gather to plant or harvest one farm at a time until all the farms in the area are finished. This communal activity is not so much a reflection of a communist past, but of a much older tradition. During Macedonia's centuries of invasions, farmers built their houses in small village clusters as protection from marauders. Each morning they left to work their outlying fields. Though the fields were family-owned, the farmers had a sense of community that still serves them well and prevented the isolation experienced by farmers and their families in other lands.

Livestock farming is also a part of the Macedonian economic picture, though generally for home consumption rather than export. The government counts 2.5 million sheep (slightly more sheep than people), 300,000 head of cattle, 5 million domestic fowl, 170,000 pigs and horses, and 80,000 beehives.

A shepherd with his goats on a farm. Agriculture accounts for over 11 percent of Macedonia's GDP.

The agricultural strengths of Macedonia are reflected in its cuisine, where lamb and beef, tomatoes and peppers, and honey-sweetened desserts are popular.

MINERALS

Besides iron and zinc, which it exports, Macedonia also produces copper, gold, silver, manganese, tungsten lead, and nickel. These resources are running low, however, and will have to be imported if their use is to continue. Macedonia still has large amounts of materials used in the building industry: marble, granite, gyspum siliceous and quartz sands, and lignite.

ENVIRONMENT

IN LAKE OHRID, Europe's oldest lake, the ancient Ohrid trout survives by the hair of its teeth in the face of overfishing and pollution. Scientists fear that it might be too late, even with a ban on fishing, to save the fish whose closest relative species died out during the Ice Ages.

The Ohrid trout is a celebrated local dish in Macedonia. Hatcheries around the lake have supported its preservation and consumption, but still the population of the 25-pound (11-kg) fish has continued to drop. Hatchery workers have been unable to collect more than half the eggs needed to keep the Ohrid trout population at its current level.

Besides the Ohrid trout, Lake Ohrid contains snails, crabs, and flat worms that have evolved and persisted nowhere else on earth. Seventeen types of fish and nearly 130 other species of animal are indigenous to the lake. Today this collection of rare marine life, having survived millions of years, is threatened by extinction.

In 1996 the Lake Ohrid Conservation Project was formed to preserve the biodiversity of the 19-mile- (30-km-) long lake. Their study concluded overfishing, both legal and illegal, from Macedonia and Albania needs to be better managed. With commercial fishing removing about 80 tons of trout a year and illegal fishing taking untold numbers of fish, the Macedonian government now proposes to ban trout fishing for five years.

Still a ban on fishing would create other problems. The tourist industry relies on the Ohrid trout to attract international fishermen, who are drawn to Lake Ohrid by the possibility of catching a 25-pound fish. Families in both Macedonia and Albania have supported themselves by fishing in Lake

Above: **A man touring Lake Ohrid's coastline by boat. The lake is a popular tourist attraction.**

Opposite: **A view of the Macedonian countryside.**

55

Ohrid. With few opportunities for employment in both countries, a ban that would damage two industries is not popular.

POLLUTION

A temporary ban on fishing also fails to address another problem that is facing Lake Ohrid: the pollution that results from raw sewage that both Albania and Macedonia dump into the lake. Nearly 200,000 people live around Lake Ohrid, and both countries are developing hotels and resorts on its shores. Water treatment facilities, neglected or nonexistent during the last half of the 20th century, are not capable of producing clean water.

AN INTERNATIONAL ISSUE

The difficulty of solving the problems of overfishing and pollution in Lake Ohrid is made more complex by the fact that the lake belongs to two countries. Isolated from each other for over 60 years, Macedonia and

Albania have not had a history of cooperation or sharing information. Still, Lake Ohrid is important to both countries, and the Lake Ohrid Conservation Project has brought the two countries together to preserve the lake for their mutual benefit. As a start, they have agreed that Lake Ohrid and its watershed constitute one ecosystem, and that all governments in the watershed must share in its management. Funds from the World Bank and other countries will be necessary to establish and regulate development and sustainable levels of fishing.

Since 1998 Macedonia has been nominally committed to the abolition of land mines and since 2001 has had a Mine Action Office in Skopje. Still, three years later, there were no laws or regulations being implemented, although both internal and international efforts had contributed to the destruction of unexploded ordnance (UXOs) and land mines.

Many people who live near the lakes depend on fishing for their livelihood.

Soldiers getting ready to destroy mines.

In 2001 the warring factions of ethnic Albanians (NLA) and Macedonian government forces signed a peace accord brokered by NATO. Under that agreement, the NATO Task Force Harvest destroyed weapons turned over by the NLA amounting to 1,054 mines and grenades and 354 other explosive devices. Still, people continued to die from UXOs as they returned to villages that were bombarded by Macedonian security forces.

NATO continued to provide assistance to Macedonia to demine roads and to locate UXOs so that people could return to their homes. With the assistance of the International Trust Fund for Demining and Mine Victims Assistance (ITF), they cleared 879 houses, 1,394 other buildings, 11.7 miles (18.8 km) of railway and roads in the last three months of 2001. The clearance resulted in the destruction of 153 UXOs and four mines. Discoveries and clearances of this sort continued throughout 2002 as other international relief groups joined the effort.

The Macedonian Red Cross developed a mine/UXO awareness program to help people recognize and avoid the dangers that persisted after the end of the conflict, especially in the north and northwest parts of the country. The danger was acute as farmers returned to their fields in spring of 2002 to plow and sow. International relief groups held information sessions in the villages, sometimes visiting homes of people who did not attend. Leaflets and posters were distributed to villagers. One of the leaflets was aimed at children and featured a cartoon character based on the famous Macedonian Shara dog, familiar to all Macedonian children.

EARTHQUAKE

It was 5:17 A.M. when the earthquake struck Skopje, a city of 200,000 people, on July 26, 1963. In the short 20 seconds that followed, 1,070 people were killed and 80 percent of the city had been destroyed. Because it was summer, and people worked early, most were awake, and they managed to flee the collapsing buildings before the walls and roofs fell in. The world's relief agencies came to the rescue of the devastated city, and a newly designed Skopje emerged from the rubble with modern buildings designed to be earthquakeproof. Today a remnant of the destroyed railroad station has been preserved in memory of those who died that morning.

MACEDONIANS

UNLIKE THE COUNTRIES of Western Europe, Macedonia and its neighboring Balkan countries have in all their political incarnations always been both multiethnic and multilingual. Perhaps it was inevitable that the ethnicity of Macedonia's people has always been a subject of controversy.

Just who are the Macedonians? Serbs have claimed them as Serbian because they had similar folk customs. Bulgaria claimed them as Bulgarian because the Macedonian language was similar to Bulgarian. Greece called them Macedonian Greeks because there had been Slavic-speaking Greeks in the area since Alexander the Great. Today's 2,050,000 Macedonians are still divided in opinion and in ethnicity. Who can claim Macedonian ethnic identity is a matter of some dispute. The claims are often based on history going back thousands of years, their accounts sometimes grounded in legend or religious documents and beliefs. But setting aside the question of who has the most right to call themselves Macedonian, several ethnic groups have a prominent presence in Macedonia: Macedonians, Albanians, Turks, Vlachs, and Roma.

Under communist rule, these groups were largely allowed to maintain their ethnic identity and religion as long as they hewed to the party line in politics and economics. This ethnic continuity has preserved traditions and religious beliefs that have in the past existed side by side.

Above: **Ethnic Albanians and Slavs in Skopje.**

Opposite: **Macedonians at a market.**

ETHNIC MULTIPLICITY

Like other Balkan countries, Macedonia's challenge is to incorporate its minority groups into a peaceful and productive society. The constitution, written in 1991, addresses the country's ethnic multiplicity: "...Macedonia is constituted as a national country of the Macedonian people which guarantees complete civil equality and permanent mutual living of the Macedonian people with the Albanians, Turks, Vlachs, Roma and the other nationalities living in the Republic of Macedonia." But Macedonia suffers from identity problems stemming from conflicts among ethnic groups with differing opportunities and national priorities.

Macedonian soccer fans cheer the national team at an international match.

Here are just a few of the matters of dispute. It is notable that these matters are not limited to Macedonia, but include the treatment of ethnic minorities in other countries as well. Greece maintains that its history predates that of the people in Macedonia who call themselves Macedonians. Macedonians maintain that this is either not true at all, only partially true, or irrelevant. Greeks maintain that Macedonians are a threat to stability because of their communist past. Macedonians maintain that the Greeks were too complicit with the Nazis. Greeks maintain that Greek Macedonians are treated badly in Macedonia. Macedonia maintains that Albanians and Macedonians are treated badly in Greece.

Albanian refugees from Kosovo have a meal in their new home in the village of Runica.

ALBANIANS IN MACEDONIA

Another element in Macedonian identity involves the presence of Albanians, a situation stemming from the 1923 creation of Yugoslavia and Albania, which set borders leaving over half of the people who called themselves Albanian outside of their newly created country. Thousands of them were

Newly promoted Albanian police officers stand at attention as the Macedonian national anthem is played.

living in the part of Yugoslavia that is today Macedonia; and like Bosnian Albanians and Kosovo Albanians, they make their presence and their demands felt forcefully. Today Albanians comprise at least 27 percent of the Macedonian population, and their rights to civil protection and power were enumerated in the NATO-brokered peace agreement of 2001 in hopes that Macedonian ethnic strife could be eased. First among the changes to the current situation was an agreement that Macedonia would amend its constitution to include all ethnic groups, not just Slavic Macedonians. In addition Albanian, or Shqip, will be recognized as a second official language in areas where Albanians constitute 20 percent or more of the population. More vaguely, Albanians were to constitute a larger percentage than previously of the police forces, and to have a degree of self-rule in areas where they are the majority. In preparation for these changes, a new census would be held before the next election to determine ethnic populations and thus award representative power.

For the Albanian Macedonians, the numbers have been in dispute since before the passing of the constitution in 1991. Though the government has proudly claimed that 76 percent of those eligible to vote did so, and that 95 percent of those voting approved the constitution, Albanians have noted that the 24 percent who did not vote were Albanian. Since then, not having approved the constitution, they have campaigned for increased representation and recognition of their needs as a minority in language and religion. Some of their demands have been met, but mistrust and dissatisfaction are ongoing.

NATO secretary-general Lord George Robertson speaks to ethnic Albanian children at a school in a village west of Skopje.

The majority of Albanians are Muslims. However, there are some exceptions: some Orthodox Christian Albanians live in a few villages around Lake Ohrid and the town of Struga, and some Roman Catholics live in Binach around Skopje. The late Mother Teresa is the best known among the Roman Catholics from Binach.

TURKS

The Turks are the second largest national minority in Macedonia. Like other ethnic groups, they claim higher numbers than the census shows, somewhere between 170,000 and 200,000. The government estimates them at around 100,000. Once there were many more, but when the Ottoman Empire fell at the beginning of the 20th century, many fled to Turkey. Under Yugoslav rule, more left after World War II. Others intermarried or simply identified themselves as Macedonians or Albanians to avoid stigma and persecution. Most Turks are Muslims.

ROMA

Turkish soccer fans support their team at a match in Skopje.

Roma probably originated in India and migrated to the Balkans during the Ottoman conquest from Asia. Most of them are Muslims. The Roma are an ethnic minority and, like most minorities in Macedonia, claim to have been undercounted in the census, which put their number at 54,000. Over 23,000 of them live in Suto Orizari, the largest Roma community in the world. More than 6,000 Roma refugees came to Macedonian as victims of warfare in Kosovo. Like the Serbs and some other refugees from Kosovo, they have not felt that they would be safe if they returned, now that the conflict has diminished. And 2,500 of them remain in the country in refugee camps and on the streets.

Roma in Macedonia, as elsewhere in the world, rarely intermarry with or mix in a communal way with people of other backgrounds. Traditionally they were gifted craftsmen and musicians, working in leather, metals, and fibers, and serving as repairmen and performing at weddings and other celebrations. Today, the Roma generally live in poverty in the cities, where they are often homeless or, at best, transients. Women and children often beg for money from tourists, though not from Macedonians, who are immune to their pleas. International efforts to improve their lot have aimed at encouraging the Roma to send their children to school, and at discouraging discrimination in opportunity and increasing regard from outsiders.

Roma children play in a slum near Skopje.

MOTHER TERESA

It is a tribute to the character of Mother Teresa and to the complexity of Albanian and Macedonian identity that Macedonia, where she was born, and Albania, home of her people, both claim her as their own.

The woman who would go on to win the Nobel Peace Prize and bring comfort and conversion to the poor throughout the world was born Agnes Gonxha Bojaxhiu in Skopje, Macedonia, in 1910. At the age of 18, she joined a convent in Ireland that did missionary work in India. At 21 she took her vows as a nun. For many years she taught at a high school in Calcutta, but it was the suffering of the poor that she saw in the streets that called to her. Her first mission was an outdoor school for the children of Calcutta's slums, relying only on volunteers and divine providence for support. In 1950 Mother Teresa founded her own order, the Missionaries of Charity, with the intention of caring for the most desolate and forsaken of people. As word of her mission and her devotion spread throughout the world, she received financial support that enabled her order to open missions in many other countries.

Mother Teresa was an inspiration to Christians who shared her desire to convert others to their faith. Many believe she will someday be named a saint. Since her death in 1997, the Vatican has recognized her ability to perform miracles, a necessary step in the canonization process. Believers feel that a woman in India who was cured of a stomach tumor on the anniversary of Mother Teresa's death was healed through prayers to Mother Teresa.

VLACHS

Since the second century, the Vlachs have been in Macedonia, making them the country's oldest ethnic group. Most of their settlements were along the Via Egnatia, the Roman trade route, where they were tradesmen and shepherds. They speak, as they always have, a Latin-based language, and call themselves Aromani, after their place of origin in today's Romania. Today they are mostly urban people, often operating successful businesses and hotels. Many do not identify themselves as anything other than Macedonian, and those that do constitute only 0.5 percent of the population.

OTHER MINORITIES

The Torbeshi are a Slavic, Macedonian-speaking population, which converted to Islam during the Ottoman period. There are also Bosnians in

Village women near the town of Prilep.

69

Macedonia, some of them since the 19th century. Throughout the period of ethnic persecution in Serbia, Bosnia, and Kosovo, refugees fled to Macedonia. By 2004 most of them had returned home to relative safety, but the enormous flow in and out of the country has left numbers unusually hard to determine.

CONFLICTS WITH NEIGHBORING COUNTRIES

It's not surprising, perhaps, that in an area of the world where invasions, conversions, and conquests were frequent and bloody, Macedonians and their neighbors had harsh words for each other. Demosthenes, the Greek orator and historian, denounced Philip II, the father of Alexander the Great, as "not only not a Greek nor related to the Greeks, but not even a barbarian from a land worth mentioning; no, he's a pestilence from Macedonia, a region where you can't even buy a slave worth his salt." Despite this evaluation of his father, Alexander the Great has always been considered a Greek hero.

Into the 21st century Greece has opposed Macedonia's use of its name and the Star of Vergina or the Vergina Sun, the 16-ray star symbol that decorates the golden larnax, a box found in a burial site in Vergina, Greece in 1977 and believed to have belonged to King Philip II of Macedon, the very man reviled by Demosthenes.

Archaeologists do not agree whether the sun was a symbol of the Macedonian state, a symbol of Philip's dynasty, a religious symbol, or simply a decorative design. Eight-pointed suns often appear in Macedonian coins and shields of that period. Eight-, 12- and (rarely) 16-pointed suns have been used as a decorative element in Greece for centuries. Macedonia conceded the use of the Vergina Sun on its flag when it joined the United Nations in 1995. An eight-pointed sun is the current design on the flag. Greece displays the Vergina Sun as the official symbol of the Greek province of Macedonia.

A painting of Greek orator Demosthenes denouncing Philip II.

MACEDONIANS

Cultural disputes with Bulgaria extend to conflict over the domain of folk songs. The 19th-century Miladinov brothers Dimitar and Konstanin published a collection of 665 songs called *Bulgarian Folk Songs from Macedonia* in 1861. Macedonian linguists have claimed that the songs are not Bulgarian, but Macedonian (and that the Miladinov brothers are also) and the collection of songs has been published in Macedonia under the title of *Folk Songs from Macedonia*. References to Bulgaria have all been carefully removed from the text. For over a century, the provenance of these songs has been an ingredient in the quarrel between the two countries.

Language has also been used as a club to coerce people into a new ethnic identity. Under Serbian rule during the 1920s and 1930s the Slavs

A group of Bulgarian women in Macedonia. Bulgarians in the country faced discrimination during Serbian rule.

Ethinic Albanian refugees arrive at a camp near Skopje.

in Vardar Macedonia were regarded as southern Serbs and the language they spoke a southern Serbian dialect. In addition to closing Bulgarian, Greek, and Romanian schools the Serbs expelled Bulgarian priests and all non-Serbian teachers, reducing the influence of their language. Bulgarian surnames ending in –*ov* and -*ev* were replaced with names with the Serbian ending -*ich*. Throughout the 20th century people living in Bulgaria and Greece exposed themselves to discrimination and danger by identifying themselves as Macedonian as their ethnicity was officially declared non-existent.

Albania recognizes a population of 5,000 Macedonians. But in the region of Golo Bardo, near the Macedonian border, there are two Slavic organizations, one Bulgarian and the other Macedonian. Each claims the Slavic population there for itself, with the Bulgarian organization saying they are Bulgarian and the Macedonian organization saying they are Macedonian. The population itself, which is predominantly Muslim, has chosen to call itself Albanian in the official census, avoiding the dispute and removing themselves from the Slavic count altogether.

The ultimate conflict over language and ethnicity finds its expression in the country's name. When Macedonia was admitted to the United Nations in 1993, its name was officially entered as "The Former Yugoslav Republic of Macedonia" in a concession to Greece, which maintained that its northern province was the only place entitled to use of the name Macedonia.

This decision did not set well with the Slav population of the new nation, who compared it to calling the United States the Former Colonies of Great Britain in North America. For years Greece was able to enforce the use of the more cumbersome name among European Union (EU) nations who require a consensus for any decision. So even though the other 11 EU countries approved, Greece successfully blocked Macedonia's use of the name and prevented its membership in some European organizations.

Graffiti on the dispute over the naming of Macedonia.

WISE OLD MEN

The folktales from Macedonia show the country's connection to many other cultures in the world. One tale, which celebrates the wisdom of old people, has versions in Germany, Romania, Serbia, Japan, and Africa. All involve old people demonstrating their wisdom, and therefore, their value to their societies. This is the Macedonian version of the story called *The Wisdom of the Old Man*:

In the old days it was customary for children to take their old fathers to the mountain to die when the village decided it was their time. There they would die of cold or be devoured by wild animals. The village would benefit by redistributing the old folks' food portion, so children who did not take their fathers to the mountain were threatened with death themselves.

Following the orders of the village leaders, a young man was taking his father to the mountain one winter night. His father's piteous weeping was too much for his heart to bear, so the young man relented and took him to his home, where he hid him in the cellar.

Throughout the winter the village received orders from the emperor to carry out a variety of tasks posed in the form of riddles. The first said, "Kill the bear that lives on the hill above the village." Since there was no bear, the villagers were confused. The young man took the riddle to his father still hiding in his cellar. The old man said, "He is talking about the rock on the top of the hill. Tell him the villagers will kill the bear, and but will wait for the emperor to come and skin it." This answer satisfied the emperor that the villagers understood his riddle.

Another order came in from the emperor. They were to collect seeds from every plant that grew in the village. Again the villagers were confused. How could they collect seeds in winter? Again the young man went to his father for advice. The old man told his son to go to an anthill where he would find the seeds already collected by the industrious ants. When the young man carried the seeds to the assembled villagers, they were astonished and pleased, but suspicious of the successes of a young man not known for his cleverness.

"Who is advising you on these matters?" they asked. And the young man confessed that he had hidden his father away in his cellar and was simply following his suggestions.

Since that day, old people are not sent to die on the mountain because everyone treasures their wisdom.

LIFESTYLE

FAMILY AND FRIENDSHIP form the fabric of the Macedonian way of life. People take seriously the need to do each other small favors and to extend and receive hospitality. These expressions of respect and affection are repeated throughout a lifetime to weave ties that bind through generations. Conversations are lively and often emotional, as people passionately express opinions based on long-held beliefs.

Macedonians welcome visitors to their homes and will always invite them to stay for a meal. To refuse such an invitation is to offer insult. Older guests are especially honored and are served food first and expected to lead conversations while others listen.

Society has gone from 90 percent rural in the mid-20th century to over 60 percent urban. Families, traditionally large, have become smaller in the urban areas as need for child labor on farms has decreased. Albanian families are an exception, and they tend to be nearly twice the size of the national average. The Orthodox Christian Church is very influential in the lives of its members, providing religious services and rituals for all of life's events. In Christian towns the church calendar provides the heartbeat with Orthodox holidays and feast days, and also with saints' days unique to each community. Even historical celebrations usually center on the church. In Muslim communities, much of the activity centers on the mosque, but the baths and the market are also central. Though the Muslim community observes the month-long Ramadan fast, many of the events throughout the rest of the year center on historical and political matters.

Above: **Worshipers inside the Macedonian Orthodox Church in Skopje.**

Opposite: **Macedonians taking a walk in Skopje.**

77

Schoolchildren reading pamphlets.

Over half the people in Macedonia live in cities, nearly a quarter of them in or around the capital city of Skopje. Though population numbers regarding ethnic composition are sometimes questioned, officially about two-thirds of the Macedonians are of Macedonian descent, a quarter are Albanian, and the remainder are Turks, Roma, Serbs, Vlachs, and other ethnic groups. The population is a youthful one, with over half the people under the age of 30. The average expected life span is 74 years for women and 70 years for men. The poverty rate has risen precipitously, from less than 4 percent in 1991 to 22 percent in 2002, with unemployment and the impact of the refugees largest among the causes.

EDUCATION

Education is available to everyone and is compulsory from the ages of 7 to 15, through the equivalent of eighth grade. Four years of high school are available, but not required. Often the high schools focus training on the economic and vocational needs of the area.

Education in Macedonia is as multilingual as its population. Primary education in the Republic of Macedonia is carried out in 1,053 primary schools, with an average class size of 25 students. The instruction is carried out in Albanian in 279 primary schools. Fifty-five schools offer instruction in Turkish to about 5,500 students, and 15 schools teach their pupils in Serbo-Croatian. Ninety secondary schools provide high school education, five instructing in Albanian, and two in Turkish. Within the schools, most children are separated ethnically, and it is unusual for them to socialize outside their groups. Still, there are those who would break down the ethnic barriers to understanding.

Ethnic Albanian university students in Tetovo.

One program called Appreciating Differences brings groups of students from ethnically mixed high schools together to encourage them to discuss multiculturalism, human rights, and stereotypes, prejudice, and discrimination.

Macedonia has about 27,000 students at two universities—the Saint Cyril and Methodius University at Skopje, and the University of Saint Clement of Ohrid at Bitola. Another 3,800 study in Tetovo at the South East European University, where most of the classes are taught in Albanian. In recent years disputes have arisen about the need for more university classes teaching in Albanian. Of people employed in Macedonia, 15 percent have college or further educational qualifications, 26 percent have completed secondary education, 30 percent have highly skilled or skilled worker's certificates.

THE STREETS OF MACEDONIA

The old and the new exist side by side in Macedonia. Medieval churches and mosques, some converted from one to the other and then back again, dot the country towns and city streets. In Skopje, modern malls in the new part of town are mirrored by the Turkish market across the river. People buy American-style fast food from food chains, or cheese pies, or

burkes, and yogurt from local street sellers. Young women in Western-style jeans and t-shirts pass observant Muslim women who cover their faces with black veils in the presence of men.

Traditionally, bargaining has played a role in Macedonian enterprises. Traders tend to start high and work their way down to acceptable levels of expected return. Macedonians see bargaining as a process and a skill, and they are very good at it. Outsiders must expect to be tested when they do business.

Tradition and unemployment keep the many cafés and coffee houses full from morning to night with men looking for company and a way to pass the time. Strong Turkish coffee, sometimes called Macedonian coffee, is the drink of choice, served in tiny cups or glasses. Increasingly in the cities, Internet cafés have sprung up, drawing in young people wise in the

Above: **Market scene in Tetovo.**

Opposite: **Women shopping in a boutique.**

High school students light candles in memory of teenager who was killed in ethnic clashes.

ways of computers and eager to keep in touch with friends and family abroad. Websites linking people of shared ethnic or religious backgrounds are popular Internet destinations. Many of them originate abroad in expatriate communities and feature chat rooms or instant messaging that keep people connected and informed.

SOCIAL ISSUES

Official documentation may say otherwise, but international human rights groups identify Macedonia as part of the main transit route from countries of the former USSR and Eastern Europe for the human trafficking of women and children into Western Europe. Additionally, evidence suggests that internal trafficking is on the rise and that Macedonia is increasingly becoming a final destination for women and children who have been sold or tricked into prostitution.

Unfavorable political, economic, and social conditions have increasingly resulted in a decline in the standard of living, reduced government services, unemployment, and rising health problems, especially among ethnic minorities. The rates of drug addiction and prostitution have risen, as have the rates of HIV/AIDS. So far, as an economically strapped economy dictates, few government programs exist to address these problems, though international agencies have addressed them. But traditional reticence in these areas has slowed the effort.

THE MACEDONIAN SHEEPDOG

Macedonia has more sheep than people, and the business of shepherding is as old as the mountains. Macedonian shepherds have a unique dog, once known only to them and to the wolves. Legend says that eagles and falcon spread heroic tales about these heroic dogs and their battles with the wild mountain beasts.

The Sarplaninac (pronounced shar-pla-NEE-natz) is an ancient dog still widely used in the mountains to protect flocks against predators. According to legend it was once unknown outside the mountains, and, in fact, it could not even be exported from Yugoslavia until 1950. Now it is a recognized breed and is sold in both the United States and Canada. Sarplaninacs are medium-sized dogs by breeding standards, about 2 feet (61 cm) tall at the shoulder and weighing between 66 and 99 pounds (30 and 45 kg) at maturity, but they seem much bigger because of their heavy bones and thick coats. Most often they are gray, but they can be any color, and in the mountains they are often mixed colors. Though they are smaller than many other sheepdog breeds, Sarplaninacs are terrifically strong with very large teeth. Their loyalty, intelligence, and initiative make them superb guard dogs. They are calm dogs generally, but they are fearless and react quickly and courageously when they sense a threat. Their speed and demeanor can easily turn back a bear or a wolf. Macedonian owners and breeders assign mystical powers to the Sarplaninac, calling it "the symbol and perfect incarnation of his noble function—to unite the world and still to build up his own identity!"

RELIGION

IN THE NINTH CENTURY, the creation of the first Slavic alphabet resulted in the spread of Christianity among the Slavic people. For the first time, a Slavonic ecclesiastical organization could use the Slavic language instead of Greek in religious services. From the flowering of Macedonian culture that grew out of the Ohrid Literary School came the Macedonian Orthodox Church.

The Macedonian Orthodox Church ministers to two-thirds of Macedonia's citizens. Most of the others practice the Muslim faith. A tiny minority is Roman Catholic or practices another religion.

MACEDONIAN ORTHODOX CHURCH

Through the centuries, the Macedonian Orthodox Church has stimulated and supported the national identity of the Macedonian people. Always in the forefront of resistance and uprisings against the Bulgarian and Ottoman Empires, it also provided education, especially linguistic and literary.

In A.D. 893 the Macedonian Orthodox Church was established in Ohrid, with Saint Clement, one of its founders, as its first archbishop. Saint Clement and Saint Naum, disciples of Saint Cyril and Saint Methodius carried on the teachings of their mentors, taking as their mission the education of their people in the Macedonian language and the establishments of schools throughout the country.

Though the Church was taken over by the Greek clergy upon the fall of the Macedonians to the Byzantine Empire in 1018, it continued to unite

Above: **A bishop gives away Orthodox crosses.**

Opposite: **An Orthodox church in the mountain resort of Popova Shapka.**

The Macedonian Ortho-
dox Church in Ohrid.

the Macedonians for over 800 years, until it was officially abolished by the
Turks in 1786. In 1945 the Republic of Yugoslavia allowed it to be revived,
though politics made membership undesirable. Once again the Church
assumed a central role in supporting a national identity.

Today's Macedonian Orthodox Church harkens back to the days of
Saint Clement's archbishopric of Ohrid. Once again it is centered in Ohrid
where it is headed by the archbishop of Ohrid and Macedonia and the Holy
Synod of Bishops, which consists of six bishops. Macedonia has more that
300 priests and monks serving 1,000 churches. Many of the churches and
monasteries are old and in partial ruin. Icons and frescoes are treasures of
the villages, where they were sometimes hidden for centuries. Today they
are shown to visitors as evidence of the skill of the craftsmen and the
tenacity and faith of the people. The oldest and most revered of the
churches are Saint Sophia and the Holy Virgin of Perivlepta in Ohrid and
the Church of the Holy Savior in Skopje. Monasteries throughout the
country are often centers of celebration for feast days and festivals.

ISLAM IN MACEDONIA

About 500,000 of Macedonia's citizens are counted as Muslim and the great majority of these are ethnic Albanians. However, Muslim activists maintain that the number of Muslims is actually much higher since the count represents only citizens and not residents. Most live in the west and the northwest, near the Kosovo and Albanian borders and in the city of Skopje. Mosques throughout the land provide architectural history of the rule of the Ottoman Empire. Most of the mosques to be seen today were built in the 15th and 16th centuries. The Isa Beg Mosque, the Mustafa Pasha Mosque, the Sultan Murat Mosque in Skopje, and the Aladzha Mosque in Tetovo are the most famous and beautiful.

Muslims in prayer in a mosque in Kumanovo.

Muslim men chatting and reading the Koran.

While the Macedonian Orthodox Church benefited from the tolerance of the Yugoslav government, the Muslims of Macedonia received treatment that was less favorable, as they were perceived to be less amenable to Yugoslav unity. Since the creation of the Macedonian Republic in 1991, mistrust has persisted between officials of the two religions. Once a part of the Islamic community administered from Sarajevo, the Macedonian Islamic community is today centered in Skopje and has around 600,000 members.

The Muslims in the Republic of Macedonia are ethnically and religiously heterogeneous. Ethnically they are the Albanians, Turks, Macedonian Muslims (Torbeshi), Bosnians, and Roma; with the Albanians in the majority. Religiously the Sunni Muslims are the majority and dominant part of the population. There are also six Sunni Sufi orders and one Bektashi Sufi order, which is the largest Sufi order in the Balkans. The Islamic community and the Islamic Dervish religious community are officially registered by the state. A bimonthly Islamic newspaper, El Hilal, is published in Albanian, Turkish, and Macedonian.

THE BEKTASHI ORDER OF DERVISHES

The Bektashi are a Sufi order of Islam that evolved in the 13th century. Some of its members become ascetics, living in communities somewhat like Christian or Buddhist monks, taking vows of poverty and pursuing religious enlightenment and ecstasy. The Bektashi are mystical in their beliefs, less concerned with the rules of Islam than with achieving spiritual peace. Their ritual of the *sema* (SEH-mah), known to outsiders as the dance of the whirling dervishes, represents a spiritual journey to reach an understanding of perfect love and to return from the journey prepared to love and serve all people, regardless of creed, race, class, or nationality.

Sufi whirling, or *sema*, is a form of meditation based on an ancient and forceful technique. Physically it involves turning the body into a spinning top as the dancer whirls in one place, spinning with eyes wide open. Dancers typically do not eat or drink for three hours before whirling,

and dance barefooted and in loose clothing. Sufi whirling is divided into two stages: whirling and resting (unwhirling). The dance usually lasts at least an hour, but it can continue for many hours or even days. As a religious ceremony, it is not usually performed for audiences.

Whirlers begin their dance with hands crossed and placed on the opposite shoulders. They rotate on their left feet in short twists, the right foot propelling their bodies around the left foot, which serves as an anchor or stabilizer. The dancers begin slowly, with the body relaxed and eyes open but only softly focused. Gradually they extend their arms, right arm held high and palm up, and left arm held low and palm down. After about 15 minutes, the dancers pick up speed, attaining their greatest speed after another 30 minutes. By this time, the dancers appear to be a fury of energy and activity, but, ideally, the spirit at the center is still. They spin until they reach such a high speed that their bodies fall softly to the ground.

Now comes the second part of the dance, the unwhirling. With eyes closed, the dancers press their navels to the ground to connect with the earth's energy, remaining still for at least 15 minutes.

LANGUAGE

LANGUAGE IN MACEDONIA, and among Macedonians in other countries, has been an integral part of the Macedonian identity. Throughout centuries of occupation, its invaders have recognized this fact and have worked hard to suppress, outlaw, corrupt, or otherwise weaken the language and thus its role. In the past century, under Yugoslav union, Serbs attempted to weaken the use of Macedonian by introducing Serbian into the schools and government. Macedonians in northern Greece were forbidden to speak Macedonian under the rule of the military junta.

The first Slavonic alphabet was created in the ninth century by Macedonican brothers Cyril and Methodius of the city of Salonica, laying the groundwork for Macedonian literacy. It was then and remains today a Cyrillic alphabet. Their disciples Clement and Naum of Ohrid went on to establish the first Slavonic university, the Ohrid Literary School, which was to graduate over 3,500 teachers, clergymen, philosophers, and other writers.

Macedonian is a unique language, though it shares some characteristics of the languages of neighboring countries including Bulgaria, Albania, and Serbia and belongs to the Slavic family of languages. Though it has been a written language since the ninth century, its first written grammar did not appear until 1946. Even without a codified grammar, however, church documents, linguistic studies, scientific treatises, literature, and translations from other languages abound in the Macedonian language.

Above and opposite: **Macedonians read the latest headlines in the newspapers.**

Election posters in Macedonian along the streets of Skopje.

The Macedonian language and alphabet are governed by rules and regularities, standardized in 1903 by Krste Miriskov. Its 31 letters are pronounced in only one way, no matter how they are combined. Another regularity governs accenting syllables: the third to last syllable always gets the accent. In shorter words, the first or only syllable is accented. These two rules make the language easy to speak.

Here are some simple words and phrases in Macedonian:

hello: *zdavo* (ZDAH-voh)

yes: *da* (DAH)

no: *ne* (NEH)

please: *molam* (MOH-lahm)

thank you: *blagodaram* (blah-GO-dah-ram)

How are you?: *Kako si?* (KAH-ko SEE?)

CYRYLLIC LETTERS

Macedonian is written in the Cyrillic alphabet.

Cyrillic	Latin	Pronounced
Аа	a	like a in father
Бб	b	as in English
Цц	c	like tz in Tzar
Чч	ch	as in English
Дд	d	as in English
Ѕѕ	dz	does not have equivalent sound in English
Џџ	dzh	like j in jungle
Ее	e	like e in men
Фф	f	as in English
Гг	g	like g in good
Ѓѓ	gj	like j in joy
Хх	h	as in English
Ии	i	like e in me
Јј	j	like y in young
Кк	k	as in English
Ќќ	kj	like cu in cute
Лл	l	as in English
Љљ	lj	like lj in million
Мм	m	as in English
Нн	n	as in English
Њњ	nj	like nj in lasagna
Оо	o	like o in gone
Пп	p	as in English
Рр	r	as in English
Сс	s	as in English
Шш	sh	as in English
Тт	t	as in English
Уу	u	like u in rule
Вв	v	as in English
Зз	z	as in English
Жж	zh	like su in pleasure

ALBANIAN

With roughly a quarter of its people Albanian, Macedonia has recognized the Albanian language as an official language of the country. In areas where more than 20 percent of the people speak Albanian, or Shqip, signage and government documents are in both languages.

Most languages evolve as parts of linguistic families, with similarities in grammar and vocabulary to older or neighboring languages, but not Albanian. Though it has a few words in common with Greek, Latin, and Italian, it is a language without relatives or ancestors.

The Albanian language has 36 letters written in the Latin alphabet, and like Macedonian, has only in the last century been codified. It has two dialects, the Gheg of the north and the Tosk of southern Albania. The literary language, however, is mostly taken from the Tosk dialect.

An Albanian man reading.

ALBANIAN ALPHABET

A	like *a* in opera
C	like *ts* in curtsy
Ç	like *ch* in church
DH	like *th* in this
E	like *e* in tell
Ë	like *u* in bug
G	like *g* in gun
GJ	like *j* in jam
H	like *h* in hope
I	like *i* in is, or like *ee* in sheep
J	like *y* in yellow
LL	like *ll* in tell
NJ	like first *n* in onion
O	like *o* in opera
Q	like *ch* in chair
RR	like a german *r* (trilled)
S	like *s* in save
SH	like *sh* in shun
TH	like *th* in think
U	like *oo* in doom
X	like *ds* in beds
XH	like *j* in jungle
Y	like French *u* (yew)
ZH	like s in vision

B, D, F, K, L, M, N, P, R, T, V, and *Z* are pronounced as in English.

OTHER LANGUAGES

Besides Macedonian and Albanian, many young people in Macedonia speak English. Older Macedonians are more likely to speak German as a second language. Though different languages, Macedonian and Bulgarian have enough in common that most people can understand both.

ARTS

THE MULTIPLICITY OF PEOPLES in Macedonia has enriched its arts for centuries. Despite the tolls taken by earthquakes, occupations, time, and poverty, the icons, architecture, music, poetry, and dance offer testimony to the talent and imagination of the Macedonian people.

ARCHITECTURE

The longtime presence of Byzantine, Turkish, and Slav peoples has left layers of civilization, and this is nowhere more apparent than in Macedonia's architecture. To a great extent the talents of the builders and craftsmen are expressed in religious buildings, sometimes, as in the cases of the Church of Saint Sophia in Ohrid, in layers of influence and history. Many of the buildings are in partial ruin. Poverty and national priorities have not always favored preservation. But dereliction has exposed former incarnations in some of the buildings, layers of painting, foundations of previous buildings, and additions constructed centuries after the primary edifice.

During the flowering of Macedonian culture in the ninth century, Christians built cathedrals and churches all over the country. The style was Byzantine, with glorious icons and altars and three- or four-nave construction. Many of these beautiful buildings still survive, some having been turned first into mosques and then back into churches. At its Christian height during the 14th to the 16th centuries, Macedonia had over 1,000 churches and monasteries, designed often in relative isolation from current trends to suit the terrain. In and around

Above: **The Church of Saint Sophia in Ohrid.**

Opposite: **Frescoes adorn the ceiling of the Monastery of Saint Naum in Ohrid.**

97

The Church of Saint Jovan Bogoslov-Kaneo overlooks Lake Ohrid.

Ohrid, for example, churches cling to cliffs and hillsides, perch on high peaks, and even overlook the lake from caves.

MONASTERIES The monasteries of Macedonia have since the ninth century been central to the lives of its people. Today there are still many working monasteries, some in Debar, Ohrid, and Prilep. The Monastery of Trekovec in Prilep was featured in the Academy Award-nominated film *Before the Rain*. In Debar is the Nunnery of Saint Gjorgj Pobedonoset, also known as Saint George the Dragon Slayer, the patron saint of England.

SECULAR STRUCTURES Byzantine secular buildings of significance were usually fortresses. Remains of the Fortress of Ohrid still stand in the city that Roman historians once referred to as a city of fortresses. The

Fortress of Ohrid is the oldest and best preserved in the country, with 18 towers and four gates remaining. Skopje Fortress is also a preserved fortress, built at least in part in 535 with stones from the ruined town of Scupi, which had been destroyed by an earthquake in 518.

OTTOMAN BUILDINGS The Ottoman Empire put an end to the construction of churches and fortresses and gave rise to a new type of settlement, based on open clusters of houses, inns, baths, and mosques. By the end of the 16th century, for example, there were more than 70 mosques in Bitola. The Painted Mosque, built in Tetovo in the 15th century, is a beautiful example of Ottoman architecture and ornamentation.

The 15th-century Painted Mosque, which locals call the Pasha Mosque.

ARCHAEOLOGY IN MACEDONIA

Macedonia's antiquities are world-renowned. Museums in many countries house historical, archeological, and artistic collections that were bought or seized from Macedonia by invaders and traders throughout the centuries. Even today nearly every turn in the road brings a view of a building, wall, or road that dates at least in part from centuries past. Remnants of the ancient cities of Stobi (Gradsko), Heraclea Lyncestis (Bitola), Lihnidos (Ohrid), and Skupi (Skopje) are still visible and sometimes central to today's cities. Many such sites now house museums, mosques, and churches. Archaeologists continue to unearth remains of civilization from the Roman and early Christian eras. Churches like Saint Panteleimon's in Ohrid date back to the times of Saint Clement in the ninth century. Islamic culture is memorialized in the monuments, bazaars, and baths of the

Right: **Ruins of a palace in the ancient city of Stobi.**

Opposite: **A Macedonian woman dressed in traditional folk costume.**

Turkish occupation. The Churches of the Holy Salvation in Skopje and Saint Jovan Bigorski in Debar draw admirers from around the world.

During the period known as the Macedonian renaissance during the 18th and 19th centuries, new monuments and churches were built. Some of the best-known icons are those in the Holy Salvation church and at Saint Jovan Bigorski's.

Besides these structural remains, which are the handiwork of master builders and mosaic artisans, there are icons, frescoes, paintings, and carvings on the walls and ceilings of many of the old buildings. Illuminated church records and writings, as well as textile work done by women, have been preserved for centuries.

FOLK ARTS

Macedonian women have for centuries been known as extraordinary needle workers. The embroidery on the national costumes of all of Macedonia's ethnic peoples identifies them by location and background. Though people rarely wear their traditional costumes in daily life any more, each area and ethnic group has its own, and they are worn on holidays and during the numerous folkloric performances. Many of the costumes for both men and women have

headpieces worked in elaborate embroidery and edged in lace. Both Muslim and Christian women covered their heads in 19th century Macedonia with a large veil made of lace or embroidered net or cotton.

Embroidery work on the costumes is organized into repeating geometric and floral motifs. The cloth is made of linen with elaborate and dense stitching in wool or cotton. The colors of the costumes have significance for both the wearer and the people who watch. Red symbolizes love, bloodshed, and fire. Brown signifies stability and steadfastness, white signifies happiness and ease, and black signifies night and mystery. A stitch known as the Macedonian stitch, with rows which alternate between left-slanting stitches and right-slanting stitches, identifies work found in other countries such as Greece and Canada as coming from a Macedonian needle worker.

LITERATURE

The Macedonian literary tradition dates from the work of brothers, Saints Cyril and Methodius, who developed the Macedonian alphabet in the ninth century. Their disciple, Saint Clement of Ohrid, translated Greek texts into Macedonian for the benefit of his people and was a gifted

writer of poetry, songs, and sermons in his own right. Other writers from the period contributed lyrically beautiful religious prayers and hymns, sermons, and elucidations of religious texts. Throughout the Middle Ages monks transcribed and illuminated religious texts and even preserved in writing some of the romances current among the people.

During the Ottoman occupation of the Balkans, Macedonian literature was largely confined to the monasteries where it was restricted to copying out known texts. The writers of the first great wave of Macedonian literature were educated in the religious tradition of the early monks, and their writing continued in the religious vein. But by then the work of Grigor Prlichev (the poems "Skenderbey" and "The Sirdar") was breaking ground for a new Balkan style of writing that celebrated folk and local heroes.

Macedonian poetry of the 20th century begins with the revolutionary poems of young men who wrote fervently as they fought occupying armies and died young. Koli Nedelkovske (1912–41) wrote *Glas od Makadonija*, a cry from the heart summoning fellow Macedonians to resist fascism.

Above: **Orthodox frescoes decorate the Church of Saint Petka in Ohrid.**

Opposite: **Saints Cyril and Methodius, inventors of the Cyrillic alphabet.**

Kosta Solev Racin (1908–43) also lived a hard short life of poverty and revolutionary resistance. His book of poetry, published in 1939, *Beli Mugri* (*White Dawns*), was forbidden by the occupying forces of his homeland, but it was passed around from hand to hand by readers who loved it for its celebration and observations of ordinary people. Its wide underground circulation had an enormous revolutionary impact, earning him the respect of his comrades. For the next four years, he continued to write and also earned the dedicated enmity of the occupiers, who pursued him for the rest of his life until his death on a mountain road in 1943. Besides poetry, Kosta Racin also wrote novels, including *The Village Behind the Seven Ashes*, *The Sleep Walker*, and *The Stubborn Heads*.

VISUAL ARTS

Macedonia has a rich artistic life. More than 260 exhibitions of work by Macedonian artists and 65 exhibitions of guests from foreign countries are organized each year. The works of the Macedonian painters Nikola Martinoski, Lazar Lichenoski, Petar Mazev, Dimitar Kondovski, Petar Hadzhi Boshkov, Vangel Naumovski, Vasko Tashkovski, and Gligor Chemerski have been exhibited around the world.

MACEDONIAN SYMBOLS

THE MACEDONIAN SUN   The Macedonian sun is a symbol of Macedonian culture that has been cherished for over 3,000 years. An eight-rayed or 16-rayed geometric rendition, sometimes called a star, has appeared on coins, costumes, flags, stamps, and religious icons. As a symbol of the ancient Macedonian Kingdom, it has been found preserved on military equipment and artworks. On medieval religious
paintings of the mother of Jesus, the Macedonian sun decorates her head covering and her gown. Hammered gold boxes and tomb paintings testify to the importance of the sun as Macedonia's symbol.

When Macedonia became an independent country in 1991, it proudly raised a flag with the 16-pointed sun. In 1992, to commemorate its independence, the Macedonian postal system issued a stamp with a picture of the flag.

THE MACEDONIAN LION   Ancient historians have left records of the presence of lions in ancient Macedonia. Among warriors and courtiers, the lion hunt was a popular pastime and competition as recorded in recovered art and artifacts. One mosaic shows a Macedonian warrior taking part in a lion hunt wearing nothing but his cape and the distinctive Macedonian hat called a *kausia* (kah-oo-SEE-yah). Macedonian kings also dressed in the lion's pelt, and an ancient coin shows a profile of Alexander the Great, his head topped with a lion's scalp.

In 338 B.C. when the Macedonians defeated the Greeks at Chaeronea in central Greece, they built a sculpture of a proud-standing lion on the battlefield. Throughout the centuries, families have identified themselves as Macedonian by incorporating the lion into their coats of arms.

LEISURE

PEOPLE IN MACEDONIA have a tradition of making their own entertainment. Every town has its own festivals commemorating historical, religious, and ethnic events both tragic and triumphant. But Macedonians are increasingly urban and youthful, and the pastimes of the 21st century, from computer dating to mall crawling, are also a part of the scene.

THE MEDIA

More than a hundred radio and television stations operate in Macedonia. Both radio and television broadcast in many languages, including Albanian, Turkish, Greek, Bulgarian, Romani, and Vlach. Macedonian television was the first to broadcast programs in Albanian. One television program, called *Nashe Maalo*, is aimed at teaching children between 8 and 12 years old the value of ethnic tolerance and nonviolent solutions to conflict. One unique use of television took place during the 2003 voluntary surrender of illegal weapons. A televised lottery was held to select prize winners from among people who turned in arms. The widespread publicity about the lottery provided an effective way to spread the news about the weapons amnesty.

The country has more than 112 newspapers and 74 other periodicals with a combined circulation of about 28 million. Three of the daily newspapers are published in Macedonian, and there are newspapers in both Albanian and Turkish that publish three times or more a week. Book publishing flourishes in Macedonia with 12 publishing houses publishing around 600 titles a year and 2 million copies. Like the other media, books appear in all of Macedonia's languages. There are 127 public libraries.

Above: **Macedonian workers watch the news.**

Opposite: **Macedonians enjoying a break in Mavrovo.**

ВРЕМЕ

ВО АВИОНСКА НЕСРЕЌА КАЈ МОСТАР

Загина претседателот Борис Трајковски

A worker in a printing factory checks a second edition of the Vreme newspaper.

There are also 133 scientific, scholarly, and specialist libraries, as well as 699 school libraries. The largest and the best known is the Saint Clement of Ohrid National and University Library, Skopje.

PHOTOGRAPHY AND FILM

In 1905 the brothers Milton and Janaki Manaki shot the first filmed material in the Balkans in their native town of Bitola and thus laid the foundations for film and photography in this region. The film industry flourished during Macedonia's days as a Yugoslav republic, partly owing to the reputation it had acquired as it built on the Manaki legacy of teaching and production. The years following independence have been difficult, as technological changes have been rapid and money scarce. Still there have been notable successes. Most recently, the Macedonian film *Before the Rain*, directed by Milcho Manchevski, was nominated for the 1995 Academy Award for best foreign film, after having previously won the Golden Lion of the Venice Film Festival.

Movie theaters are everywhere in Macedonia, showing a wide range of films in many languages and from many countries. Macedonian moviegoers are accustomed to seeing experimental and foreign films as well as dubbed and subtitled versions of Hollywood blockbusters.

THEATER

Ten professional theater companies are active in Macedonia, presenting more than 1,000 performances each year. There is a Theater of the Nationalities in Skopje, consisting of Albanian and Turkish drama companies. There are also Romani theater companies.

The most successful theater companies are the Drama Theater and the Macedonian National Theater, both in Skopje, the National Theater, Bitola, and the Pralipe Romani Theater. These companies have been winners of a large number of the highest awards in the former Yugoslavia and also of many international prizes and acknowledgments. The Theater of the Nationalities with its Albanian and Turkish drama companies has also participated in many national and international theater festivals and has received high praise.

The founder of the modern Macedonian theater is Vojdan Chernodrinski (*Macedonian Blood Wedding*, 1901). Goran Stefanovski is the author whose plays have been most frequently performed. There have been 70 productions of his plays in Macedonian, Serbo-Croatian, Slovene, English, French, Russian, German, Albanian, Turkish, Hungarian, Polish, Slovak, Romanian, and Greek.

MUSIC AND DANCE

The Macedonian National Theater is also home to an opera and a ballet company. The first opera by a Macedonian composer, *Goce*, by Kiril Makedonski, was performed on May 24, 1954. The first Macedonian ballet was *A Macedonian Story*, by Gligor Smokvarski, performed in 1953. Macedonia also has a philharmonic and five other professional orchestras.

There are 99 amateur cultural, artistic, and educational associations throughout the country. Of these, 21 perform or present programs in Albanian, Turkish, or Romani. Each year local organizations present about 10,000 performances, concerts, evenings of light music and folk music,

Skopje-born Romani singer Esma Redzepova is an internationally acclaimed performer.

exhibitions, and other events. These organizations are central to preserving the traditional dances and music of Macedonia, passing on traditional knowledge about songs, dances, and musical instruments.

A group of Macedonian folk dancers.

FOLK DANCING AND MUSIC

The *teskoto* (TESH-koh-toh), or the hard dance, is the traditional dance performed by the men of Macedonia. Like circle dances in many cultures, the *teskoto* is a dance known to most of the men in the country. It is a dance that acknowledges the sorrow and difficulty of life and the awakening of the Macedonian national spirit. Facing each other in a circle, the men hold their hands high in the air and move to the slow, stately beat of a large cylindrical drum, called a *tapan* (TAH-pahn), and the *zurla* (ZUR-lah), a double-reed instrument like an oboe, with a keening moan. As the music accelerates, the men dance faster. The dance ends when the oldest dancer leaps onto the drum and kneels as the drummer slows the beat to a doleful stop.

The *teskoto* is Macedonia's most famous and beloved dance. It is often performed for visitors by people dressed in their traditional ethnic or national costumes. But it is just as likely to be performed spontaneously by a group of people at a wedding, a holiday feast, or a street fair. With many young men leaving home to pursue work in other countries, it is sometimes performed as a farewell.

Macedonian dancers are usually accompanied by the *tapan* and one or more wind instruments. The *kaval* (KAH-vahl) is a pipe without a

Opposite: **Basketball players from Croatia and Macedonia in a match in Ohrid.**

Below: **A man plays the *zurla* at a wedding ceremony.**

mouthpiece. The player blows across the edge of the opening, like blowing on a bottle. The length of the pipe determines the *kaval*'s tone; the longer the pipe, the deeper the tone. Macedonian bagpipes, *gajda* (GAHJ-dah), contribute a characteristic drone to many festivities, and the lovely two stringed-lute called a *tambura* (TAHM-boo-rah) can often be heard in the background. Often the music is provided by Roma musicians.

SPORTS

Sports activities take place in more than 1,500 clubs with about 150,000 active members. The most popular sport is soccer, followed by basketball, handball, volleyball, wrestling, swimming, and karate.

Like soccer fans everywhere, Macedonians play soccer wherever they can, in the street or in the clubs. They are also loyal fans to their teams. The Vardar Skopje soccer team has a history that stretches back to Macedonia's days as a Yugoslav republic when the team was a one-time champion of the federal football league and winner of the Yugoslav Cup. Since then they have competed in the Balkan Cup, the Central European Cup, the UEFA Cup, and the European Cup-Winners' Cup.

Participants in a wrestling competition in Skopje.

In 2004 runners carried the Olympic flame through western Macedonia on its way to the Summer Olympic Games in Athens. While it was a part of Yugoslavia, Macedonians competed as part of the Yugoslav team, but since independence it has competed under its own name. In the summer games of 2004, it had athletes competing in swimming, wrestling, kayaking, canoeing, shooting, and boxing. Mogamed Ibragimov won the first Olympic medal for Macedonia since its independence when he brought home the bronze medal in wrestling from the 2000 Olympics in Sydney.

The Macedonian sport which has won the greatest number of prizes is wrestling. The wrestler Saban Trstena was the winner of the gold medal at the 1984 Olympics in Los Angeles and of the silver medal in Seoul in 1988. His colleague, Shaban Sejdiu, was the bronze medalist at the Moscow and Los Angeles Olympics. Several Macedonian boxers have been European champions, and the Balkanec Wrestling Club from Shtip was the Club Vice-Champion of Europe. Six other Macedonian sportsmen (Ace Rusevski, boxing; Redzhep Redzepovski, boxing; Stojna Vangelovska, basketball; Blagoja Georgievski, basketball; Blagoe Vidinik, soccer; and Branimir Jovanovski, shooting) have won medals in the Olympic Games.

OUTDOOR RECREATION

Macedonia's tiny size and varied landscape gives its people opportunities to take part in an amazing variety of outdoor activities. Swimming, water skiing, hiking, bicycling, and boating of all kinds are very popular in the mountain and lake districts. Divers in Ohrid can explore a sunken village. Even people in the cities are rarely more than a half hour's drive from the mountains where they can climb, camp, hunt, or just sit and watch the sun move behind the mountain. Mountaineering is the most popular outdoor sport, not surprising in a country that is 80 percent mountainous. Throughout the country, mountain hostels cater to the needs of mountaineers, providing dormitory sleeping for tired climbers.

Children have fun in a park in Skopje.

The sport of caving, or speleology, in Macedonia has an international reputation. Just outside Prilep, on the way to Modriste, is an area of caves and underground tunnels where people once lived in complex communities dependent on each other for defense. The tunnels are today being studied, like others around the country, for their archaeological significance.

Winter activities include skiing, ice fishing, and winter camping. January and February are the best skiing months, and, like hikers, skiers are never far from a mountain.

As conflicts in the area have diminished, tourism has begun to bring in outsiders who see potential in the beauty and variety of the Macedonian outdoors. They have brought with them an appetite for things such as paragliding and orienteering that may be new to the area but have been quickly accepted.

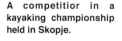

A competitior in a kayaking championship held in Skopje.

HOT SPRINGS

Macedonia has eight hot springs that provide medicinal baths. The water bubbles up from underground, passing through the minerals that give it its healing powers. Calcium, lime, and sulphur are the minerals of healing, and the smell of sulphur is a characteristic of the waters and the area around them. Some of the baths that have been built to use the water are only available to people by doctor's prescription. Others are open to all and are beautiful examples of Turkish architecture. The Bansko Turkish Hot Springs near the Bulgarian border is one of the original Turkish baths. The Banjiste baths near the Albanian border are fed by three hot springs. In the morning, the baths are used for medicinal purposes and for physical therapy, but in the afternoon they are open to all.

THE MANAKI BROTHERS

Janaki Manaki (1878–1954) and his brother Milton (1880–1964), Macedonian photographers, were the first cameramen in the Balkans and its historians. Macedonians mark the beginning of their cinematic history with their establishment of the Studio for Art Photography in Bitola in 1905. For the next few years they won international renown, traveling and exhibiting in Paris, Vienna, and London. In London Milton saw his first movie camera and found a new direction and medium. With a Bioscope camera he founded cinematography in Macedonia.

The Manaki brothers began their cinematic record of Macedonian life with a film of their 114-year-old grandmother, a weaver in their hometown. Along the way they recorded the lives and work of other weavers, weddings, religious rituals and celebrations, ethnic festivals and customs, and, importantly, the reprisals of the Turks against the Macedonians following the Ilinden uprising. To show their films, they opened a movie theater.

In still photography, the brothers made a record of the first half of the 20th century. Their photographs preserve the images of the Balkan Wars and World War I, and continue to and beyond the liberation of Macedonia from the Nazis in 1944. They show soldiers in new uniforms with heads held high and soldiers in rags who turn their faces away.

FESTIVALS

MUSIC FESTIVALS CELEBRATING folk music, drama, fine arts, and ethnic traditions occur throughout Europe every summer. Many of the musicians and players travel all summer performing at festivals throughout the continent. One of the best of the music festivals has taken place in Macedonia since 1961 in the city of Ohrid. Each summer from mid-July to mid-August, performers drawn from more than 40 countries appear in about 40 concerts and plays. Over its history the festival has presented more than 30,000 local and international artists.

On Saint Spas Day in June, the tiny village of Dolneni holds its Festival of Folk Instruments and Songs. From all over Macedonia and other countries in Europe, musicians and listeners descend for an international music festival. Musicians dressed in national and ethnic costumes perform centuries' old songs on traditional instruments. Bagpipe, horns of all sorts, and stringed instruments ring out to the delight of an audience that is often as international as the performers.

Several international cultural events and festivals are held each year in Macedonia. The best known are the Ohrid Summer Festival of Music and Drama, in which renowned musicians from around the world take part, and the Struga Poetry Evenings, which every year gather some 200 poets from about 50 countries. Ohrid is also the place where the Balkan Festival of Folk Song and Dance is held. Veles organizes traditional meetings of writers from the Balkan countries in honor of the founder of modern Macedonian literature, Kosta Racin.

Above: **A musician from Cuba performs at the Skopje Jazz Festival.**

Opposite: **Archbishop Stefan, head of the Macedonian Orthodox Church, holds a service at Christmastime.**

Skopje is host to the World Cartoon Gallery, the May Opera Evenings, and the Open Youth Theater Festival.

EASTER

This is the most important holiday for Christians in Macedonia, celebrating the resurrection of Jesus and his taking upon himself the sins of the world's people. The week before Easter is celebrated as Holy Week, and tradition guides each day. On Wednesday, people in Christian homes dye eggs red. They rise early to do this because of a belief that eggs painted before dawn hold special powers to protect the household against evil. On Friday they do no hard work, not even cooking. They attend services in the church

A Macedonian girl celebrates New Year's Eve in Skopje.

and fast in remembrance of the day Jesus died. Each person brings a flower and takes one home to bring good health. Saturday is the day of the funeral. Just before midnight people come to the church carrying candles and red eggs. They parade three times around the church while singing. At midnight the church bells resound, and the priest greets the people with the words "Christ is risen." The people respond, "He is risen indeed," and the mourning period is over. Sunday is the day of celebration, and people go early to the church to receive holy communion. The celebration continues for three more days.

ILINDEN UPRISING

The Ilinden, meaning Saint Ilijah's Day, uprising was set for August 2, 1903. According to legend, Ilijah was taken to heaven in a chariot of fire. Organizers of the uprising found the symbolism of his death and his day to bode well for their rebellion. Throughout Macedonia, people revolted against the Ottoman Empire that day, and on August 3 proclaimed

themselves the Republic of Krushevo. After only 10 days, the uprising was quelled by Turkish troops outnumbering the rebels 16 to one. The hideous reprisals visited on the Macedonian population remain in memory and in photographs. Though the independent Republic of Krushevo had only a 10-day life, the revolutionary effort that brought it about remained a part of Macedonian identity throughout the 20th century. Today, August 2 is celebrated as a national holiday.

FOLK CUSTOMS

Folk customs are cherished in Macedonia as a tribute to the past and a link to people who, though separated by borders, share the same beliefs and practices. In summer, festivals are held throughout the country in towns large and small, from Skopje to Ohrid to Tetovo.

Some of the holidays celebrated by Macedonians are related to the harvest cycle, like Saint Trifun's Day, when people go out to prune the grape vines in preparation for the new growth.

Duhovden, or Spirits' Day, is celebrated by Christians throughout the country on three days in June usually beginning on a Sunday. The dates vary from year to year, but the first day is the most important. On that day people clean the graves of their ancestors and cover them with walnut leaves. People bring food and drink to the church, sharing with their fellow parishioners in honor of the dead.

Saint Jovan's Day is celebrated at the monastery in Bigorski. The first day of this two-day holiday is a day of fasting. In one house in the village, a woman makes bread with flour bought with money from the church. When it is ready, she carries it to the monks at the monastery while the people from the village celebrate. In the evening the people sit down together for a great feast, which the women have been preparing throughout the day. The priest blesses the water, and the people take it home with them believing that it now has the power to heal. The evening is filled with music and dancing.

GALICHNIK WEDDING Near the city of Mavrovo is a tiny mountain village called Galichnik, a place with few year-round residents. But every year in July the village comes to life as visitors drive up a winding road into the mountains and then walk the final distance, mostly uphill in usually very hot weather, to attend the Galichnik Wedding. Here, high in the mountains, the poets say, is the place where time begins and ends.

For more than a hundred years, the conflicts that shook the Balkans have made this area inhospitable for the young men working in the trades and crafts. As they do today, many emigrated, relocating to countries with more secure economies where they earned money to help support their families at home. Though they lived abroad, Galichnik retained a hold on their hearts, and most wanted to marry girls from home.

A traditional bridal dance during the Galichnik Wedding festival in western Macedonia.

In order to maintain relationships migrants began to come home at the same time every year, on Saint Peter's Day, the 12th of July, and it became a tradition that anyone who wished to marry would have their wedding then. Often there would be as many as 50 weddings in Galichnik on Saint Peter's Day, with every wedding party supplying their own music: two drummers playing the *tapan* and two playing the *zurla*. The celebrations lasted as long as a week.

Today the Galichnik Wedding has one bride and groom, chosen to be the prince and princess of the festival, and just one pair of *tapan* and *zurla* players. Dancing and music, traditional costumes and customs all come together at the Galichnik Wedding as people from around the country and around the world gather to refresh their memories and their spirits, responding to the words of an old folk song: "Wherever you may be, on Saint Peter's Day you come home." The music echoes throughout the mountains for the two days of the festival. As at so many Macedonian festivals, men dance the *teskoto*, the slow dance they call "the hard one" in recognition of the sorrowful and difficult course of Macedonian history.

STRUMICA CARNIVAL The end of February brings the Strumica Carnival, a festival of masks that has been celebrated in Strumica since at least 1670. Traditionally, as in many Christian countries, the carnival marked the beginning of Lent, which ushered in a six-week period of fasting for Christians. Today it is a more secular festival to bid farewell to winter and welcome spring.

At the traditional Masked Ball, celebrants crown the carnival prince and princess. Thousands of masked people from Macedonia and other European countries march in the procession to the Masked Ball. The masks are brilliantly colored and fireworks accompany the festivities.

The next day is the children's carnival and a whole day and night of festivities including dancing, storytelling, and music with traditional costumes. The carnival concludes with visits to the homes of engaged women, who receive their masked guests and accept gifts and best wishes.

A Macedonian girl in Strumica celebrates an Orthodox Christian holiday where dance rituals supposedly chase away evil spirits.

FOOD

MACEDONIA'S TRADITIONAL CUISINE shows the influence of the many ethnic groups and countries that have contributed to its culture. Stuffed grape leaves show a Greek influence, *burek* (BOO-reck) with its filo dough crusts and various fillings resembles dishes known by other names throughout the Balkans. Easter breads and other pastries associated with holidays appear in the cuisines of many countries that share religious beliefs and customs.

Traditional food includes bread, soups, stews, lamb kebabs, stuffed vegetables, moussaka, and minced meat dishes such as *kjebapchinja* (kye-BAHP-chee-nya) and meatballs. Meat (pork, chicken, lamb, beef) and fish are served with rice, pasta, and vegetables (eggplant, beans, cucumber, mushrooms, peppers, potatoes, and tomatoes). Dairy products include yogurt and feta, a white salty cheese. Desserts eaten in Macedonia are fruit salads, puddings, cakes, and pastries. Strong Turkish coffee, sometimes called Macedonian coffee, is served in all homes and restaurants and cafés. Wine, beer, and soft drinks are produced locally. The wines of Macedonia have been garnering international praise.

Excellent fresh fruits and vegetables are available in season. Though their season is short because of a dearth of cold-storage facilities, when they are available, they are fresh and flavorful for that very reason. Most are grown on small family farms without chemical treatment. Macedonia is especially well-known for its variety of delicious peppers, which are featured in many traditional dishes.

Above: **Moussaka is a traditional dish in Macedonia.**

Opposite: **A fruit stall in Macedonia.**

127

One of the most popular desserts in Macedonia is called baklava. This heavy, honey-drenched dessert is made mostly in winter, about two to three times a year by the average Macedonian family. Different fillings are used between the layers of filo dough featuring walnuts, grapes, and yogurt. Another, simpler favorite is *sutlijash* (SUHT-lee-yash), or rice pudding.

And then there are the fast foods of the West. Shopping malls in Skopje and other cities feature pizza, hamburgers, and tacos like any mall in North America or Western Europe.

The words for meals in Macedonian are *dorucek* (DOE-roo-chek, breakfast); *rucek* (ROO-chek, lunch); *vechera* (VEH-che-rah, dinner); and *uzina* (OO-zhee-nah, afternoon snack).

A grocer in Tetovo.

PASTRMKA (TROUT)

The Ohrid Trout is rare and delicious, and available only in Macedonia and Albania in Lake Ohrid. Here is a recipe for preparing trout that has been used to prepare the Ohrid trout for centuries. This recipe makes four servings.

4 trout
$^1/_2$ cup flour
$^1/_3$ cup olive oil
$^1/_3$ cup butter
1 teaspoon paprika
1 lemon
$^1/_3$ cup sour cream

Wash the fish and dry it. Sprinkle with salt. Heat the olive oil and butter. Dredge the fish lightly in the flour and put it in the pan. Fry over medium heat for about 3 minutes on each side. Remove the fish from the pan. Stir the paprika and juice of the lemon into the pan drippings and cook for about 5 minutes. Stir in the sour cream and pour the sauce over the fish. Serve immediately.

POLNETI PIPERKI (STUFFED PEPPERS)

Macedonia's peppers are world famous. Here is a recipe for a dish known to all Macedonian cooks. It serves six to eight as a side dish.

8 medium green, yellow, or red bell peppers
3 tablespoons butter
4 small onions, finely chopped
2 small green peppers, finely chopped
1 clove garlic, minced
1 cup chopped or ground ham
1 1/2 cups chopped tomatoes
salt and pepper
3 to 4 cups bread crumbs
2 eggs
cracker crumbs for topping

Cut a thin slice from the stem end of each pepper. Scrape out the seeds and white membrane, and wash the peppers. Drop them into boiling, salted water and parboil for 5 minutes. Drain well and pat dry. Melt the butter in a heavy skillet. Add onions, garlic, and chopped pepper and saute until limp. Add tomatoes, ham, and salt and pepper to taste. Simmer for 15 minutes. Remove from heat. Stir in the bread crumbs and eggs. Stuff the mixture into the pepper shells and stand them up in a baking pan. Sprinkle the tops with cracker crumbs. Bake in a 350 degree oven for about 25 minutes or until the stuffing is firm and lightly browned on top.

TAVCHE GRAVCHE (MACEDONIAN BEANS)

Also known as "overdone beans," this recipe serves six to eight people as a side dish.

1 pound (0.5 kg) dried beans
1 onion, chopped
$^1/_2$ cup olive oil
2 or 3 pieces dried red pepper
salt and pepper
fresh parsley and mint

Wash the beans and let them stand in a cooking pot in water overnight. Bring the beans to a boil. Drain the beans and, once again, put them in the pot with enough water to cover them by about an inch. Add the capsicum. Continue to cook the beans until they are soft but not mushy. Drain the beans if there is too much water left. The cooking time will depend on the kind of beans you use and how old they are, but it will be at least an hour. Fry the chopped onion and paprika in cooking oil, then add this to the beans. Put everything in a baking pot. Stir in parsley, mint, pepper, and salt. Bake until the beans are a little bit softer, but not dry—about $^1/_2$ hour.

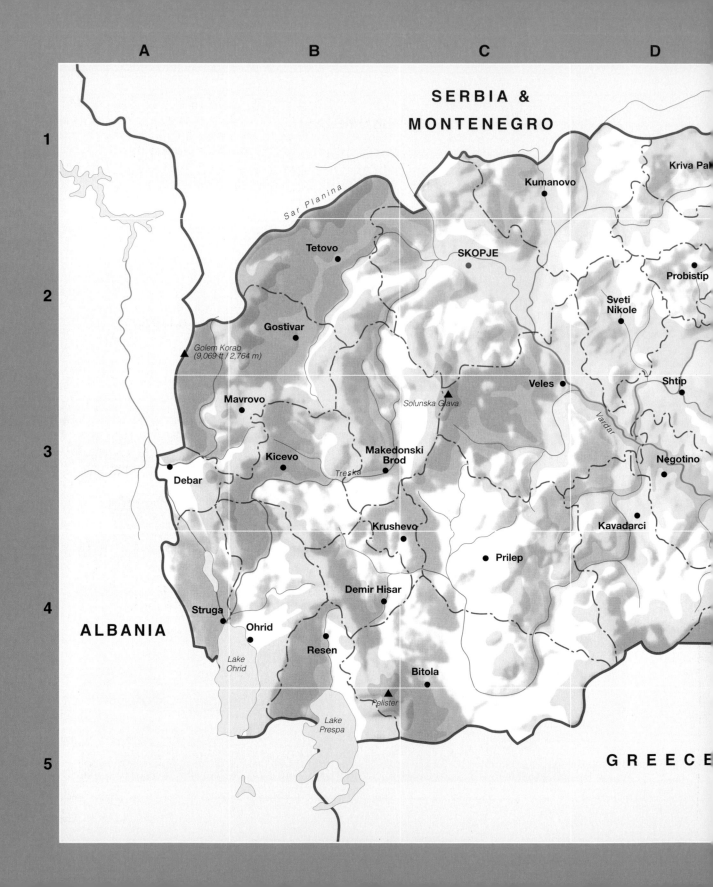

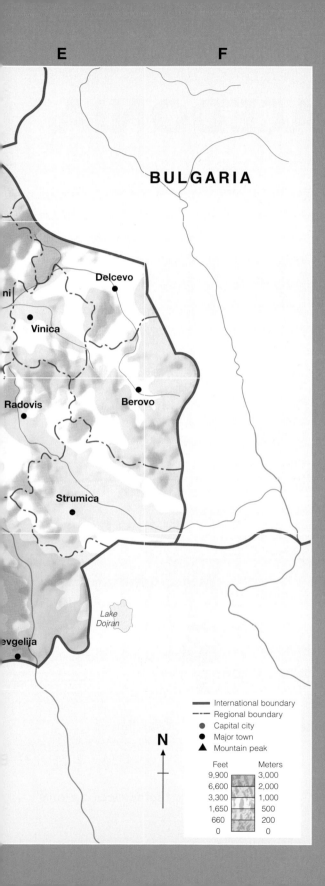

E   F

BULGARIA

Delcevo

ni

Vinica

Radovis   Berovo

Strumica

Lake
Dojran

evgelija

N

—— International boundary
-·-·- Regional boundary
● Capital city
● Major town
▲ Mountain peak

Feet	Meters
9,900	3,000
6,600	2,000
3,300	1,000
1,650	500
660	200
0	0

MAP OF MACEDONIA

Berovo, E3
Bitola, C4

Debar, A3
Delcevo, E2
Demir Hisar, B4
Dojran, Lake, E4

Gevgelija, E4
Golem Korab, A2
Gostivar, B2

Kavadarci, D3
Kicevo, B3
Kocani, E2
Kriva Palanka, E1
Krushevo, C4
Kumanovo, C1

Makedonski Brod,
  B3
Mavrovo, B3

Negotino, D3

Ohrid, B4
Ohrid, Lake, B4–B5

Pelister Park, B5
Prilep, C4
Prespa, Lake, B5
Probistip, D2

Resen, B4
Radovis, E3

Sar Planina, B1
Shtip, D3
Skopje, C2
Solunska Glava, C3
Struga, A4
Strumica, E3
Sveti Nikole, D2

Tetovo, B2
Treska river, B3

Vardar river, D3
Veles, C3
Vinica, E2

133

ECONOMIC MACEDONIA

Farming

🍃 Tobacco

Manufacturing

🥫 Food Processing

🌊 Hydroelectricity

✈ Metals

🛢 Oil Refining

▮▮ Textiles

🏭 Thermoelectric Plants

Services

✈ Airport

🧍 Tourism

Natural Resources

🐟 Fishing

⬛ Lignite

ABOUT
THE ECONOMY

OVERVIEW

Prior to claiming independence in 1991, Macedonia was the least developed of the Yugoslav republics, producing only 5 percent of the total output of goods and services. As an independent nation, several factors slowed Macedonia's economic growth: UN sanctions on Yugoslavia, which was one of its largest markets; a Greek economic embargo; and Macedonia's lack of a working economic infrastructure all hindered growth until 1996 at which point GDP began to rise, a trend that continued through 2000. Then unrest in the Albanian community weakened the economy, which shrank 4.5 percent in 2001. Growth recovered slightly in 2002 to 0.9 percent, and became stronger, at 2.8 percent, in 2003. Average unemployment of 33 percent is Macedonia's most critical economic problem.

GROSS DOMESTIC PRODUCT (GDP)

$13.81 billion (2003 est.)

LABOR FORCE

860,000 (2003 est.)

CURRENCY

1 Macedonian denar (MKD) = 100 deni
USD 1 = MKD 47.2 (November 2004)
Notes: 10, 50, 100, 500, 1000, 5000 denars
Coins: 50 deni; 1, 2, 5 denars

POPULATION BELOW POVERTY LINE

30.2 percent (2002 est.)

GDP SECTORS

Agriculture 11.3 percent, industry 32.1 percent, services 56.6 percent (2003 est.)

UNEMPLOYMENT RATE

36.7 percent (2003 est.)

NATURAL RESOURCES

Iron ore, copper, lead, zinc, chromite, manganese, nickel, tungsten, gold, silver, asbestos, gypsum, timber

AGRICULTURAL PRODUCTS

Rice, tobacco, wheat, corn, millet, cotton, sesame, mulberry leaves, citrus, vegetables, beef, pork, poultry, mutton

EXPORTS

Food, beverages, tobacco, miscellaneous manufactures, iron, steel

IMPORTS

Machinery and equipment, chemicals, fuels, food products

EXPORT PARTNERS

Germany, Italy, Greece, Croatia, United States, The Netherlands

IMPORT PARTNERS

Greece, Germany, Yugoslavia, Slovenia, Bulgaria, Italy, Turkey

CULTURAL MACEDONIA

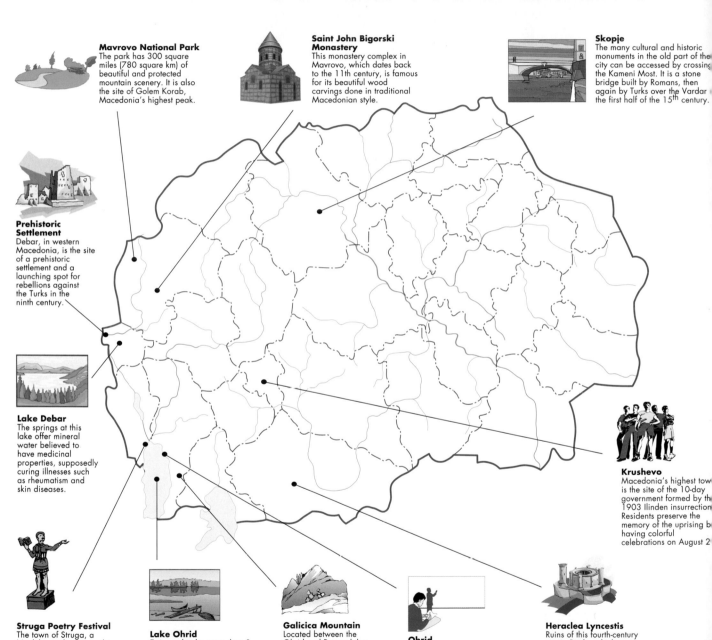

Mavrovo National Park
The park has 300 square miles (780 square km) of beautiful and protected mountain scenery. It is also the site of Golem Korab, Macedonia's highest peak.

Saint John Bigorski Monastery
This monastery complex in Mavrovo, which dates back to the 11th century, is famous for its beautiful wood carvings done in traditional Macedonian style.

Skopje
The many cultural and historic monuments in the old part of the city can be accessed by crossing the Kameni Most. It is a stone bridge built by Romans, then again by Turks over the Vardar the first half of the 15th century.

Prehistoric Settlement
Debar, in western Macedonia, is the site of a prehistoric settlement and a launching spot for rebellions against the Turks in the ninth century.

Lake Debar
The springs at this lake offer mineral water believed to have medicinal properties, supposedly curing illnesses such as rheumatism and skin diseases.

Krushevo
Macedonia's highest town is the site of the 10-day government formed by the 1903 Ilinden insurrection. Residents preserve the memory of the uprising by having colorful celebrations on August 2.

Struga Poetry Festival
The town of Struga, a Neolithic settlement on the Via Egnatia, is now known as the capital of Macedonian poetry and home of the yearly Struga Poetry Festival.

Lake Ohrid
Estimated to be more than 3 million years old, the lake is the fourth oldest in the world. It is also the deepest lake in Europe and home of the Ohrid trout.

Galicica Mountain
Located between the Ohrid and Prespa lakes, the mountain has underground and underwater caves with stalactites and stalagmites.

Ohrid
The city, which has UNESCO's World Heritage status, is the site of the first university in the Balkans, the Ohrid Literary School.

Heraclea Lyncestis
Ruins of this fourth-century city in Bitola, which was founded on the Roman road the Via Egnatia, include a theater, basilicas, a forum, and intricate floor mosaics.

ABOUT THE CULTURE

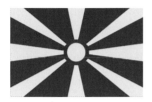

COUNTRY NAME
Republika Makedonija; The Former Yugoslav Republic of Macedonia

GOVERNMENT TYPE
Parliamentary democracy

CAPITAL
Skopje

NATIONAL HOLIDAY
Uprising Day, August 2 (also known as Saint Elijah's Day and Ilinden)

POPULATION
2,071,210 (July 2004 est.)

AGE STRUCTURE
0-14 years: 21.5 percent
15-64 years: 67.8 percent
65 years and over: 10.7 percent (2004 est.)

ETHNIC GROUPS
Macedonian 64.2 percent, Albanian 25.2 percent, Turkish 3.8 percent, Roma 2.7 percent, Serb 1.8 percent, other 2.3 percent (2002 Macedonian government figures)

RELIGIONS
Macedonian Orthodox 70 percent, Muslim 29 percent, other 1 percent

LANGUAGES
Macedonian 68 percent, Albanian 25 percent, Turkish 3 percent, Serbo-Croatian 2 percent, other 2 percent

LEADERS IN POLITICS
President Branko Crvenkovski (since May 12, 2004)
Prime Minister Hari Kostov (since May 14, 2004)

LEADERS IN THE ARTS
Saint Clement of Ohrid (840--916) and Saint Naum (835–910)—founders of Ohrid Literary School and codifiers of Macedonian language and alphabet
Janaki (1878–1960) and Milton Manaki (1882–1964)—photographers and filmmakers
Konstantin Miladinov (1830–62)—poet
Kosta Racin (1909–43)—poet

HISTORIC FIGURES
Alexander III, aka Alexander the Great (356–323 B.C.)—king and military commander
Saints Cyril (Constantine) (A.D. 827–69) and Methodius (A.D. 826–85)—brothers and Christian teachers
Grotse Delchev (1872–1903)—leader of Macedonian fight for independence
Mother Teresa (Agnes Gonxha Bojaxhiu) (1910–97)—humanitarian and Nobel Peace Prize winner

TIME LINE

IN MACEDONIA	IN THE WORLD
	753 B.C. Rome is founded.
c.653 B.C. King Perdiccas I establishes the Macedonian Kingdom.	
336–323 B.C. Reign of Alexander the Great. Macedonia reaches the peak of its military power.	
323 B.C. Alexander dies, dynasty collapses	
215–167 B.C. Macedonia falls under Roman rule.	**116–17 B.C.** The Roman Empire reaches its greatest extent, under Emperor Trajan (98–17).
	A.D. 600 Height of Mayan civilization
A.D. 855–86 Brothers Cyril and Methodius create the Slavic alphabet and spread Christianity.	
969 Macedonians rebel against Bulgarian authority and establish medieval Macedonian state.	**1000** The Chinese perfect gunpowder and begin to use it in warfare.
1018 Macedonian Empire falls under Byzantine rule.	
1395 Macedonia falls under five-century Turkish rule.	**1530** Beginning of trans-Atlantic slave trade organized by the Portuguese in Africa.
	1558–1603 Reign of Elizabeth I of England
	1620 Pilgrims sail the *Mayflower* to America.
1767 Abolition of Archbishopric of Ohrid	**1776** U.S. Declaration of Independence
	1789–1799 The French Revolution

IN MACEDONIA	IN THE WORLD
	• **1861** The U.S. Civil War begins.
	• **1869** The Suez Canal is opened.
1903 • The Ilinden Uprising	
1912 •	
First Balkan War	
1913 •	
Second Balkan War. Macedonian territory split among Bulgaria, Serbia, and Greece	• **1914** World War I begins.
1915 •	
Bulgaria occupies Macedonia.	• **1939** World War II begins.
1944 •	
Proclamation of the Macedonian state	• **1945** The United States drops atomic bombs on
1946 •	Hiroshima and Nagasaki.
Adoption of the first constitution of the People's Republic of Macedonia	• **1949** The North Atlantic Treaty Organization (NATO) is formed.
	• **1957** The Russians launch Sputnik.
	• **1966–1969** The Chinese Cultural Revolution
1967 •	• **1986**
Archbishopric of Ohrid restored; proclamation of Macedonian Orthodox Church	Nuclear power disaster at Chernobyl in Ukraine
1991 ••	**1991**
Referendum on a sovereign and independent state	Break-up of the Soviet Union
1993 •	
Macedonia admitted to the United Nations	
1995 •	
Macedonia becomes member of Council of Europe.	• **1997** Hong Kong is returned to China.
	• **2001** Terrorists crash planes in New York, Washington, D.C., and Pennsylvania.
	• **2003** War in Iraq

GLOSSARY

Aegean
Formerly, the southern part of Macedonia; now part of Greece.

autocephalous
Independent, or having its own head.

balkanize
To knowingly assemble a group of people who have differing, usually incompatible, goals.

basilica
A Christian church built on Roman design with a central nave.

fresco
A painting, usually religious, executed on wet plaster walls and ceilings.

Gordion Knot
A seemingly insolvable puzzle or problem, taking its name from the knot Alexander the Great untied to demonstrate his fitness to lead.

Ilinden
Saint Elijah's Day, and the August 2 anniversary of the 1903 uprising.

Kameni Most
The bridge across the Vardar in Skopje that separates the old from the new city.

Macedoine
An Italian or French salad of mixed fruit, named for the ethnic mix in Macedonia.

pastrmka (PAH-sterm-kah)
Macedonian trout.

Pirin
Formerly, the western part of Macedonia; now part of Bulgaria.

privatization
Giving or returning property to the people that once belonged to the government.

Sarplaninac (shar-pla-NEE-natz)
Macedonian sheepdog.

Shqip
The official Albanian language.

Tertiary
The era dating from 63,000 years ago when plants and animals first appeared on the earth.

Titov Vrv (TEE-tohv VERV)
The second highest mountain in Macedonia, named after Marshal Tito.

UXO
Unexploded ordnance; mines and bombs set or dropped during armed conflict that remain on site after the conflict ends.

Vardar
The area named after the river that flows through it, today constituting the country of Macedonia, once part of Yugoslavia.

FURTHER INFORMATION

BOOKS

Fildes, Alan and Joann Fletche. *Alexander the Great: Son of the Gods*. Los Angeles: J. Paul Getty Trust Publications, 2002.

Fox, Robin Lane. *Alexander the Great*. New York: Penguin Books, 1994.

Greenway, Paul. *Eastern Europe*. Victoria, Australia: Lonely Planet Publications, 2003.

Nardo, Don. *Philip II and Alexander the Great Unify Greece*. Enslow, 2000.

Phillips, John. *Macedonia: Warlords And Rebels In The Balkans*. New Haven: Yale University Press, 2004.

Poulton, Hugh. *Who are the Macedonians?* Bloomington: Indiana University Press, 2000.

Roberts, J.M. *Illustrated History of the World*. New York: Oxford University Press, 2001.

Wood, Michael. *Alexander the Great*. New York: Penguin, 2004.

MUSIC

Dances of Macedonia and the Balkans, Adam Good, 2002.

Traditional Music From Macedonia, Strune, Arc Music, 2003.

VIDEOS

Before the Rain, Polygram Video, 1995

In the Footsteps of Alexander the Great, PBS Home Video, 1998.

*Macedonia: The Land of a Go*d, Volumes 1 and 2, Kultur Video, 1995.

WEBSITES

Alexander of Macedon. www.alexanderofmacedon.org

Cultural Macedonia. www.culture.org.mk/default-e.htm#tuka

Government of the Republic of Macedonia. www.gov.mk/English

Governments on the WWW: Macedonia. www.gksoft.com/govt/en/mk.html

Macedonia FAQ. faq.macedonia.org/quicklinks/quicklinks5.html

Reality Macedonia. www.realitymacedonia.org.mk/web/firstpage.asp

Republic of Macedonia. www.b-info.com/places/Macedonia/republic

Skopje Online. www.skopjeonline.com

BIBLIOGRAPHY

Danforth, Loring M. *The Macedonian Conflict: Ethnic Nationalism in a Transnational World*. Princeton. NJ: Princeton University Press, 1995.

Evans, Thammy. *Macedonia: The Bradt Travel Guide*. New York: Globe Pequot, 2004.

Kaplan, Robert D. *Balkan Ghosts: A Journey Through History*. New York: Vintage, 1993.

West, Rebecca. *Black Lamb and Grey Falcon: A Journey through Yugoslavia*. New York: Penguin, 1940.

Winchester, Simon. *The Fracture Zone: A Return to the Balkans*. New York: Harper Collins, 1999.

INDEX